Julie Smith (signature)

Wake 'Em Up!
Super-Charge Your Student Engagement

Julie Smith

The title's lame,
   the cover is worse

      but it's done

First Edition

and our names are
   in print again ☺

Thank you for being you

♥ (NFA)

To order, contact:

The Part-Time Press

P.O. Box 130117

Ann Arbor, MI 48113-0117

Phone/Fax: 734-930-6854

https://www.Part-TimePress.com

First printing: December, 2020

© 2020 The Part-Time Press

ISBN: 978-0-940017-55-9 (paperback)

Printed in the United States of America

Praise for *Wake 'Em Up*

"Experience tells us that engagement among teacher, students, and content is essential to effective teaching and learning. Why is that? How can we create more engaging classrooms for ourselves and our students? Wake up to Julie Smith's lively and brisk review of the reasons and ready-to-use resources—shared with the heart and mind of a truly engaging teacher and colleague."—*Elizabeth (Beth) J. Stroble, Ph.D., Chancellor, Webster University*

"Building upon a decades-long career as an educator and a passionate media literacy advocate, Julie Smith has managed to curate personal experiences, pedagogical and cognitive scholarship and practical advice in her latest book on student engagement. Recognizing that the 21st century classroom is populated by digital natives whose technology skills and expectations of learning are acutely different from what many educators have grown accustomed to, the author offers an accessible and easy to implement mix of pedagogical observations and specific strategies to increase student engagement in the classroom. This is a great read for any college instructor who is struggling to find an accessible 'how to' guide to make students comfortable, willing to participate and get involved in both the traditional and virtual learning environment."—*Elza Ibroscheva, Ph.D., Associate Provost, Southern Illinois University-Edwardsville*

"We could call this 'student engagement,' but in an age where every meeting is now performing for an audience to keep them interested, *Wake 'Em Up* is a roadmap for engaging audiences. Julie Smith gives us easy-to-read, easy-to-implement techniques delivered with authority and occasional impish charm."—*Judd Slivka. Director of Digital Content, 12News Phoenix, former faculty, University of Missouri School of Journalism*

"Julie Smith has an uncanny ability to let her personality shine through her words while offering realistic and joyful opportunities to make students take notice. After reading her work I was set and ready to take my teaching up a notch!" — *Kim Darche, Adjunct Professor and Instructional Coach*

Preface

Today's college students are not eager to sit in classes and listen to dry lectures. They crave involvement, voice, authenticity and creativity. In other words, they crave *engagement*.

Engagement is beneficial for both the faculty member and the student. Engagement increases student retention, success and enjoyment. A reputation for being an engaging instructor can also make the difference in a dynamic and competitive higher education job market.

This book was written as a "how-to" guide for engaging instruction, but it also provides the science behind why engagement is so important. You will find tech tools as well as "old school" methods within these pages, and you are encouraged to experiment.

QR codes are included for the websites mentioned. Many smart phone cameras now will send you straight to the website when a photo of the QR code is taken, no QR code reader necessary.

You will also find resources for connecting with other teaching faculty who are interested in bringing engagement strategies to their classrooms. After all, an experienced instructor is an excellent resource!

Consider this book a jumping off point on your journey into creating an exciting, engaging and successful classroom. Are you ready? Let's go!

Julie Smith

Table of Contents

How To Get the Most Out of This Book...

One important tool of the book is the use of icons to highlight important information for the reader.

Keys to Success: Whenever you see this icon, you'll want to take special note because these are tried and true tips to improve your classroom engagement.

Caution Light: Whenever you see this icon, you'll know that other successful instructors have discovered what NOT to do while teaching.

In addition to the icons, an index has been compiled for ease of use, and we have included a section about copyright fair use guidelines. There are chapters on student engagement techniques with and without technology, as well as tips for creating engaging classroom discussions. The table of contents is very detailed to get you to the topic that most interests you at the moment.

> **This is your quick reference for engaging teaching. You may use this book as a manual, a guide, or for professional reading. It contains practical and informative tips to assist you. It is written in a user-friendly manner for your convenience. Enjoy it and GOOD TEACHING.**

CHAPTER 1
WHY ENGAGE? WHY I WROTE THIS BOOK AND WHY YOU SHOULD READ IT

A family friend finished her first semester of college teaching. Since she wasn't used to having a winter break, she told me that she was actually feeling a bit guilty. I suggested that she take the time to "jazz up" her lessons and make them more engaging. Her response became the impetus for this book.

"I did fifty-nine PowerPoints last semester and I am not going to retire them."

Fifty-nine PowerPoint presentations: I can't judge her. Can any of us judge her, really?

My first semester of university teaching included many more PowerPoint slides than my students would have liked. But eighteen years of working to more effectively engage millennials and adult students have shifted the paradigm for me. I have learned that for my classes to be engaging – and therefore more successful – they need to be more about my students and less about me. And definitely less about PowerPoint slides. We've all been there: the classroom where the professor stands at a lectern and drones, the conference where the keynote speaker reads slides, or the staff meeting where we are handed an agenda and fake pay attention.

To be clear, there will always be a place in higher education for a well-delivered, interesting and passionate lecture, but faculty who want to better and more comprehensively engage their students need to stop viewing the lecture-with-slides model as the norm. Research shows that humans learn better when we are fully engaged, and that lectures aren't a foolproof engagement technique. This book will serve as guide for you.

> ## "Boredom is rage spread thin."
> ## – Paul Tillich, Philosopher

Student Engagement Cannot Wait

There's more to engagement than just having students participate actively in class. Engagement is a mindset, whereby you as the educator become less of a "sage on the stage" and more of a facilitator of student learning. Physiology professor Macknight (2016) writes, "To provide quality education what we deliver must be engaging and authentic. By engaging, we mean that students are involved in the learning process and not simply passive receptacles for the material."

If you ask someone to describe a typical college classroom, he or she will most likely describe a room with the professor in front and students sitting quietly in rows. Indiana Jones taught archeology in that same setting. The crew from "Animal House" slept through classes in rooms designed the same way. Despite the fact that this is the image that conjured up in popular culture, there isn't any evidence that this is actually the most effective way to teach. "Evidence is lacking that (lecturing) should be the only instructional approach used, especially when too many college students passively sit in classrooms while pretending to pay attention" (Lumpkin, Achen and Dodd, 2015).

Doyle writes that "Creating learner-centered environments is the most important thing that faculty can do to optimize student learning" (2008). Learner-centered environments are just what they sound like: a space where the students are the center of the activity, not the instructor. Yet think of the university classroom: the desk/lectern/professor is at the front of the room with furniture or desks that are anchored to the floor facing the professor. The set-up of most college classrooms makes student-centered learning a compelling challenge for the faculty member.

Tackling the challenge is worth it, however. After all, what is the point of education?

"We want students to remember the concepts and skills that we teach them (retention) but we also want students to take what they have learned and apply it to new, unrelated contexts" (Cook and Klipfel, 2015).

Our jobs as instructors are more important than ever – which is why we need to meet our 21st Century students where they are, rather than where we might be. Choy, Goh and Sedhu point out in their article "How and Why Students Learn: Development and Validation of the Learner Awareness Levels Questionnaire for Higher Education Students," "The activities carried out in the classroom and reasons why students learn will determine the type of learning that takes place" (2016).

Hardman (2016) agrees: "Research with university students shows significant levels of retention and understanding being achieved through active approaches to learning...compared to lecturing." In other words, when we stop viewing the lecture as our default delivery method of information and explore other more student-centered instructional methods, our students will be more successful. When you learn to utilize classroom engagement techniques, you will do more than simply delivering course content. Teaching scholar Jean Mandernach writes that student engagement is essential: "Student engagement is an integral component of a successful learning experience" (2015).

 High levels of engagement positively impact student retention. Think of it this way: which kinds of instructional techniques are more likely to make a student feel more involved, and therefore more a part of the class and larger university culture? Research by Crosling, Heagney and Thomas (2009) asserts that: "What goes on in the teaching and learning programme is significant in student retention." (Jankowski, 2016) says, "Students who are actively engaged are more satisfied, more likely to complete, and more likely to learn."

Even if student retention issues are not on your radar, retention is on the radar of every university administrator. "In the current competitive and globalized higher education market, the reputational fall-out of low student retention and high student attrition figures can be damaging for institutions" (Crosling, Heagney and Thomas, 2009). Student retention rates have enormous financial implications for all colleges and universities.

One of the universities where I teach has launched a program for first year students called "Learning Communities." The freshmen live and take several classes together. Even an uncomplicated program like this can have an impact on retention. "Student engagement in educationally purposeful activities during the first year of college had a positive, statistically significant effect on persistence, even after controlling for background characteristics, other college experiences during the first college year, academic achievement, and financial aid" (Kuh et. al 2008).

Student backgrounds, majors or socio-economic levels have less bearing than you may think on how well engagement strategies can improve the educational experience. In addition, when students enjoy college and do well, they stay in school.

The research shows us quite clearly that student engagement is a significant aspect of enriching the classroom experience. So why aren't more universities requiring their faculty to scale back the lecture model and adopt more student-centered learning strategies? For starters, faculty simply might not know how to identify and integrate student-centered learning strategies into their courses. After all, while faculty members have advanced degrees in their subject areas, the majority have never taken a course in education techniques. To complicate matters, non-tenured faculty may have no access to their college's instructional development resources. Yet, as higher education research has demonstrated, this professional development is crucial to both the student and the faculty member.

"Because faculty are often untrained in the art and science of teaching, they typically are not familiar with how to proceed or fulfill their instructional goals" (Dunneback and Therrell, 2015). Jankowski places the responsibility of this training on the shoulders of administrators: "Higher education needs to provide the support for faculty to undertake such tasks" (Jankowski, 2016). However, professional development training for faculty can fall between the cracks or, for non-tenured faculty in particular, be viewed by administrators as superfluous. This means all faculty—including non-tenured faculty—must be pro-active in the pursuit of their own development books, materials and opportunities.

Before we get into the specifics of how you can improve student engagement, let's reflect on how students learn and what makes a classroom experience memorable for them. Why do certain engagement strategies work on so many levels to improve learning?

Simple Brain Science Behind Engagement

Don't wait "until next semester" to engage your 21st Century Learners and don't worry! You won't need a degree in neuroscience or physiology to understand how your students absorb and remember the course materials you present in your classes. On the other hand, knowing how the brain works when students are engaged in their learning will help you choose and implement your instructional strategies much more effectively. Thus, understanding the importance and function of engagement must start with an understanding of how students learn and what makes information memorable. This knowledge will help you create and integrate course materials, lessons and experiences in the classroom that will improve your students' comprehension and learning.

The good news for instructors is that cognitive psychology has found that almost all human brains share important similarities in terms of how they absorb and process information (Cook and Klipfel, 2015). That doesn't mean, however, that the process of memory-making is not complex.

Forming new memories is not as simple as inserting a memory chip into a computer or putting a memory into a particular mental "filing cabinet." In fact, memories are actually chemical changes that take place in between the neurons, or synapses, of the brain. Neuroscientists estimate that there are over 100 trillion of these synapses in a typical human brain.

One of the mysteries of memory is how we can forget phone numbers or state capitals, but always remember how to drive or brush our teeth. Neuroscience researcher John Byrne claims that this is because there are two types of memories: declarative and nondeclarative. Declarative memories relate to facts and events, nondeclarative memories relate to skills and habits (2017).

The location of the memory within the brain depends on the type of memory involved. Although the hippocampus is the part of the brain considered to hold many short-term memories, neuroscientists believe that these short-term memories are eventually dispersed throughout the brain where they become long-term memories. Research suggests that this happens while we sleep.

So how does the brain decide which memories are stored, and which are forgotten? What can we as instructors do to help students move memories from short-term storage to long-term habits and skills?

Riley (2016) writes that "Understanding the science of learning should be part of the knowledge that all educators possess as they begin their careers." Yet, for many of you, the first time you teach in a university classroom you may do so without the basic knowledge of how to deliver material in a way that will make it memorable for the students. Another challenge you will face is that today's students learn much differently than you did when you were in school. The learning advice you heard (and possibly even heeded!) isn't as useful in the multi-media classroom. "For as much as we learn in class, the old-school advice on studying - maintain a strict ritual, block out all distractions, find a quiet study space, 'hole-up' with the books - is limiting. If the brain is a learning machine, it's an eccentric one, and does not take orders so well" (Carey, 2015).

The brains of your students are much different than the brain you had when you were in college. How so? Your students have grown up in a different world that is more stimulating than could have possibly have been imagined thirty years ago. On the other hand, the brain's mechanisms related to memory work the same. "College students' ability to disregard or filter out unpleasant information is stored in the prefrontal cortex, the section of the brain that houses working memory" (Lei, Donoso, Foutz, Lasorsa and Oliver, 2011).

This is the "executive function" – the part of the brain that keeps our students organized and helps them decide whether to attend class or skip. The prefrontal cortex is a faculty member's doorway into a student's memory.

Data scientist Paul King suggests that there are specific ways instructors can push through that prefrontal cortex: repetition, surprise, emotional impact or positive outcome (2017). In other words, engagement can lead us into a student's long-term memory, which is "Basically nothing more than the record left by a learning process" (Fathima, Sasikumar and Roja, 2012).

"You'll find boredom where there is the absence of an idea."
– Earl Nightingale, Author

Mary Stormon-Flynn (2011) suggest that the most effective educators are aware of the brain's role and utilize that knowledge to craft lessons. "Being cognizant of the brain's role in absorbing, processing and storing information allows educators to see the value in scrutinizing the type of material they are presenting and how they are providing it will be more meaningful for students." This isn't to say that once faculty learn about brain functions they automatically become better teachers. There are countless variables that affect the learning that takes place in a classroom. Research shows that "Learning is a highly complicated process that depends upon interactions among various individual and environmental factors" (Wang, Su, Cheung, Wong and Kwong, 2013).

There are factors, however, that educators can control. For example, as a faculty member you can learn about brain functions, study what makes material memorable, then work to make your classrooms more student-centered and engaging. It's important to see yourself as more than just someone who passes along bits of information. The British educational visionary Sir Ken Robinson agrees, when in his TED Talk he says "You're not just there to pass on received information. Great teachers do that, but what great teachers do is also mentor, stimulate, provoke, engage. You see, in the end, education is about learning. If there's no learning going on, there's no education going on. The whole point of education is to get people to learn" (Robinson, TED Talk, 2006).

While you can control as many variables in your classroom as possible, sometimes that isn't sufficient to enhance student retention of the course material. Acknowledging that your students are not jars to be filled with facts, figures and ideas is the first step to improving student learning and their overall recall of the course materials. "We now understand better than ever before how people actually learn and we should design our materials to enhance that learning" (Macknight, 2016). That being said, Lave reminds instructors that: "Only learners can learn. Teachers cannot do it for them or make students learn, making teaching a complicated activity focused upon creating an environment in which students can and do learn" (2011).

Like some of you, unfortunately, the records left from my first year of teaching do not include many fond memories. When I began teaching, I had a mental image of how my classes would go. Sadly, reality was much different. According to the *Chronicle of Higher Education's* Katharine Mangan, I wasn't the only new hire who may have felt "bamboozled." "Faculty members are often bamboozled into thinking that students are going to remember all these pearls of wisdom we've tossed at them" (Mangan, 2017).

I knew next to nothing about learning environments, and yet they played an enormous role in how my students remembered the material. I knew nothing about formative assessments, engagement techniques, learning styles or environments. I knew my subject matter. I also knew that I had a huge textbook that I was expected to get through by the end of the semester. Instructional research shows that this was not a recipe for student success. "Rushing through material to cover greater amounts of course information does not build strong neural connections in the brain" (Lei, Donsos, Foutz, Lasorsa and Oliver, 2011).

Through the years I feel that my efforts have improved, but my teaching is still a work in progress. We are reminded that "Students must want to learn and decide what they wish to remember." (Lei, Donoso, Foutz, Lasorsa and Oliver, 2011). However, our efforts can increase these odds. After all, "Cognitive psychology literature also indicates that people tend to remember what they pay attention to" (Cook and Klipfel, 2015).

Research shows that "Increasing students' cognitive engagement has been demonstrated to increase their information retention" (Cook and Klipfel, 2015).

Want to improve student retention? Increase your classroom engagement.

Making Material Memorable

If research shows that we tend to remember what we pay attention to, then logically we should attempt to increase student attention. Many professors, however, still consider the traditional lecture as the most effective way to relay information. This is beside the fact that most students consider lectures to be akin to watching paint dry. Why? "The traditional approach to the lecture will concentrate on the presentation of information without seeking to stimulate the audience" (Short and Martin, 2011).

This is not to say that you should never lecture. Research suggests that college instructors should attempt different and various peda-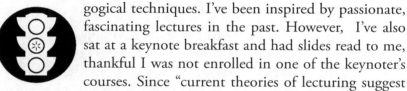gogical techniques. I've been inspired by passionate, fascinating lectures in the past. However, I've also sat at a keynote breakfast and had slides read to me, thankful I was not enrolled in one of the keynoter's courses. Since "current theories of lecturing suggest that the teaching methods employed should aim to inspire the student rather than simply provide them with knowledge" (Short and Martin, 2011), we cannot ignore this issue.

Some might say that lectures are necessary for today's constantly-plugged-in 21st Century student. Perhaps they need the skill of focusing and taking notes from an effective, well-delivered lecture. "Few people would disagree that getting students more engaged in their education is a worthy goal. But with so much focus today on

 **"Boredom is to be controlled by, rather than to control what, you do." – Heraclitus, Philosopher**

active learning, some faculty members feel like they're expected to jump through too many hoops to keep their students entertained. There's something to be said, they argue, for getting multitasking, hyper-connected students to sustain attention on a full-length, well-crafted lecture" (Mangan, 2017).

I don't disagree with this. However, the key words in that statement are "well-crafted." Lectures aren't always bad. Bad lectures are always bad. Dublin professor J. Hardman's study concluded that "There is a widespread problem with student passivity and disengagement in the classroom, which is largely attributed to poor and restrictive tutor-student interaction" (Hardman, 2016). If an instructor wants to avoid passive students, the instructor needs to avoid passive lectures. The change from "sit and get" classrooms to those that are student-centered can be shocking for some. "Students find participating in active learning activities an invigorating break, interesting, interactive and enjoyable" (Lumpkin, Achen and Dodd, 2015).

Student-centered activities shift the focus of the classroom away from the instructor and toward the students. "Students express how learning activities effectively varies the pace of classes, thus making them more enjoyable" (Lumpkin, Achen and Dodd, 2015).

Paulo Freire, in his book *Pedagogy of the Oppressed*, critiqued teacher-centered learning as the "banking method" of education, which sees students as merely vessels that need to be filled with knowledge provided by the instructor. When your classroom is student-centered, it is more about them and less about you. Research shows that this type of classroom environment is more effective.

When the instructor acts as a facilitator in the learning and includes the students in the process, "There is a body of evidence from the U.S. (and in other countries) that the more students interact with other students and staff, the more likely they are to persist" (Crosling, Heagney and Thomas, 2009).

There are dozens of ways to implement student-centered learning into your classroom. Be prepared for something interesting to happen: you will learn, too.

First Time Teacher Revelation #27

CHAPTER 2
BENEFITS OF INCREASED ENGAGEMENT

Student success, increased memory and retention are not the only benefits of increased classroom engagement. You will find that your enjoyment of the classroom experience increases as well.

The Success of Your Class

All too often, the success of a class, student and instructor are simply measured by the grades that the students have earned in the class. However, there are many other kinds of information that need to be considered when measuring the success of a class: student engagement, student retention and instructor satisfaction also need to be considered.

Students who are engaged with the course materials stay in the class—increased student retention. "Student engagement in educationally purposeful activities during the first year of college had a positive, statistically significant effect on persistence, even after controlling for background characteristics, other college experiences during the first college year, academic achievement, and financial aid" (Kuh, Cruce, Shoup, Kinzie and Gonyea, 2008).

Students who are engaged with course content also learn the course content. These two outcomes are strongly correlated with an active classroom.

Instructor satisfaction is another key in determining the success of your class. "Faculty are the linchpins to student success. They are at the center of student success not just as individual pieceworkers in increasingly large classrooms, but as a collective, engaged in various departmental and organizational initiatives to enhance student achievement" (Rhodes, 2012). Faculty matter in facilitating student engagement and success (Umbach and Wawrzynski, 2005).

"The enemies of human happiness are pain and boredom." – Arthur Schopenhauer, Philosopher

Instructors who create active learning course content and classrooms will be more engaged with the course material. Why? You'll move beyond the hour long "sage on the stage" lecture format and be working in a dynamic, challenging environment where course materials are created and analyzed (higher-level thinking goes on). The instructor is engaged, working alongside the students, creating and analyzing.

Improved Evaluations

It's no secret that student evaluations play a role in the hiring, promotion and maintenance of faculty. Student evaluations play a larger role in the careers of non-tenured faculty than they do in those of tenured colleagues.

It's also no secret that student evaluations can be a tricky business: a student can anonymously judge us without any repercussions or objectivity. Student evaluations can range from glowing to spite-filled. Yet in many universities, they are the primary source of quantitative data on teaching faculty. Should we, as faculty, fear them or embrace them? We don't have that choice. Research shows that skepticism can be appropriate here, even if evaluations are viewed as gospel by administrators. "A final concern is that faculty almost universally express great cynicism about student evaluations and about the institutional commitment to teaching quality when student evaluations are the dominant measure of quality" (Wieman, 2015).

The impact of student evaluations serve as an impetus for many reluctant faculty members to try a more student-centered approach. "But, the good news is that, irrespective of the staff, the students coming now into the system are aware of how things could be done better. In the end, it is student opinion that will result in the changes that tertiary institutions must make to stay relevant and deliver the best learning environment for the students, who will create the better world that we all believe education can provide" (Macknight, 2016).

Benefits of Increased Engagement

The significant impact of the evaluations can sometimes be paralyzing for teachers curious about trying new things. "Faculty are often reticent to take any perceived risk with their instruction in fear of how their students will rate them or potentially comment negatively on the (evalution) form. Such fear or reticence often constrains faculty from implementing or even considering new teaching/learning methods" (Dunneback and Therrell, 2015).

My personal experience demonstrates that students appreciate an instructor who tries engagement techniques more than they appreciate one who stands at a lectern and reads slides. That effort is recognized in course evaluations. When you engage your learners in a student-centered classroom, the course evaluations will become your allies in a way that will surprise you. Which brings us to...

Market Conditions

All faculty—including non-tenured faculty—face competition for courses and jobs. Therefore, it makes sense for all faculty to make themselves as valuable as possible as employees. Two ways a university measures the value of a faculty member? Course evaluations and student retention rates.

 "When it comes to how teachers may hinder learning, one student wrote about 'lack of engagement in class, unmotivated professor, constant note-taking instead of conversation and lack of creativity'" (Dunneback and Therrell, 2015). This is *not* how you want your class evaluated. Market conditions do not favor the unmotivated, uninspired employee.

Classroom Relationships

Research shows us that relationships matter in the classroom. Stormon-Flynn writes that, "When strong positive feelings are present, students can retain what they learn" (2011).

An instructor who engages students rather than talking at them has a much better chance of developing relationships with those students. Discussions happen. Names get learned. Personalities emerge. Memory of material increases. Willis writes in the book *The Neuroscience of Joyful Education* that "Neuroimaging studies and measurement of brain chemical transmitters reveal that students' comfort level can influence information transmission and storage in the brain" (2007).

Relationships lead to connections. Think of your connections in your field. Now imagine connecting one your students with a contact of yours. This can change a student's life. If you don't know your students, you can't do that. Joseph Heider explains that "To some extent, engagement with students begins with teaching them things they are interested in and/or making connections between the course and students' lives—their current lives or as they imagine their future employment. This effort takes teaching and learning beyond mere knowledge transfer" (2015).

Plus, it's simply more enjoyable when you know your students. It's difficult to get to know them from behind a lectern.

Student Success Rates & Retention

Severiens, Meeuswisse and Born did a study comparing student-centered classes and lecture-based classes. They discovered that active learning leads to more student success than those based strictly on lecture (2015). When classrooms becomes student-centered rather than instructor-centered, student success increases. When students are successful in school, they stay in school.

Increased Love of Teaching

All faculty are experts on their subject matter and some teach without the constraints and pressure of researching and writing. We love teaching. What better way to demonstrate your love of teaching than to try new ways to make it more engaging?

When I talk about trying new ways to engage my college students, some might suspect that I do it out of love and affection for them. That's only partly true. It's actually more fun for me. Kohn's article "Feel-Bad Education: The Cult of Rigor and the Loss of Joy" backs me up here: "Learning does not come from quiet classrooms and directed lectures, but from classrooms with an atmosphere of exuberant discovery" (2004).

Is there a rule that says learning has to be boring and dull? Why can't we bring a joyful spirit to higher ed? After all, are joy and learning mutually exclusive? I don't think so, and neither does Willis: "There are no neuroimaging or brain wave analysis data that demonstrate a negative effect of joy and exuberance in classrooms" (2007).

At this point, you are wondering if you "have time" for engagement strategies. You do. You must. You've spent time preparing PowerPoints and lectures. You can spend that same amount of time and produce something amazing.

It's not additional effort. It's different effort. An absolutely necessary effort. Not just for enjoyment, retention and improved memory, but for actual student grades. "Student engagement in educationally purposeful activities had a small but statistically significant effect on first-year grades. Specifically, a one-standard deviation increase in "engagement" during the first year of college increased a student's GPA" (Kuh, Cruce, Shoup, Kinzie and Gonyea, 2008).

Engaging classrooms can actually lead to students mastering higher-level cognitive skills. Cook and Klipfel discovered that, "Meaningful active learning methods engage with higher-level cognitive activity, including exercises that require finding, evaluating and using information. Students are asked to take concepts they learn in class and meaningfully engage with them. This is in contrast to more traditional teaching styles, such as lecturing" (2015).

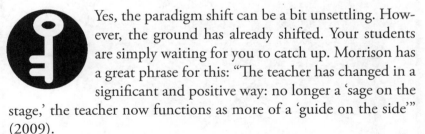 Yes, the paradigm shift can be a bit unsettling. However, the ground has already shifted. Your students are simply waiting for you to catch up. Morrison has a great phrase for this: "The teacher has changed in a significant and positive way: no longer a 'sage on the stage,' the teacher now functions as more of a 'guide on the side'" (2009).

Wenglisnksly takes it one step further: "Changing the nature of teaching and learning in the classroom may be the most direct way to improve student outcomes" (2000).

The fear of trying new things is understandable. Morrison writes that "Teachers will cling to conventional, status quo approaches to education so long as they cannot imagine alternatives" (2009).

Are you ready to wake up your classroom with alternatives?

CHAPTER 3
Non-Tech Engagement Strategies

Even if you consider yourself a luddite when it comes to technology, there are dozens of engagement tools and techniques that require no technology whatsoever. These "old-school" methods are a great way to get your feet wet. Remember that engagement is a process and that no one is expecting you to do all of these at once. However, these techniques are an excellent place to start.

Relationship-Related Strategies

Greet Them at the Door

This one sounds almost too easy, yet it can make a world of difference. Think of the tone this sets for your students: instead of you rushing into the room as class is about to begin, you stand in the hallway and greet each student as they arrive. Right away, students will know that your course will be different.

If you want your classes to be more student-centered, then you need to be present for them as they enter, unlike a conductor who comes in right before the performance begins. "Seemingly irrelevant things that we process through our bodies and our physical senses do affect our states of mind, mostly without our awareness" (Lobel, 2014).

I've had students write in evaluations that my simple act of standing in the hallway before class put them at ease and made me seem more accessible. It also provided me an opportunity to chat with them as they arrived. This led to another big engagement benefit: classroom relationships. Research tells us that this can have an effect on learning: "The quality of social relations involved could become as much a focus for planning and organization as any attempt to advance the intended outcomes for student learning" (Kahn, 2013).

One day a tenured colleague whose office was across the hall from my classroom suggested that I was "making every other teacher look bad" by greeting students at the door. I wonder what his course evaluations look like?

Have Music Playing

Think of what a typical college classroom looks like before class begins. Students stare at their phones in a silent room. So here's another technique that sets the tone, leads to relationships and can even be content-related.

I always have music playing in the room before class. How does this lead to relationships? Well, I typically play 80s New Wave music and show a photo of that day's band on the screen. They learn something about my quirky music taste and it leads to conversations. Students usually say something like "My mom loves this band" or "Have you heard this remake?" These are student interactions that would not happen in a silent room.

I also take a photo of the screen and Tweet out that "band of the day" and (if possible) tag the band. Yes, we have been re-Tweeted by several New Wave 80s bands. My students will call me a liar, but they love it when that happens.

I teach media courses, so I am fortunate that there are many songs I can play before class that are content-related. "Dirty Laundry" by Don Henley is all about the news media. "Too Much Information" by The Police is all about how we are inundated with data. Our students love music, so why not hook them before class even starts? *The Chronicle of Higher Education* agrees: "We should start class with a deliberate effort to bring students' focus to the subject at hand" (Chronicle, 2016).

Edweek takes it one step further, claiming that "Something magical happens when music is added to the classroom experience" (*Edweek* site, 2016). In what ways can music set the tone for your class, before class even begins?

Learn Their Names & Encourage

Do you ever notice how some people say they are "terrible with remembering names?" Some people do seem to have a skill with name recollection. But claiming that remembering names is impossible is a cop-out. There are dozens of tips and tricks online to help the recall of names.

I take a very basic approach in class, however. On the first day, I have students decorate card stock name tents and they are required to keep that name tent on their desk the first four weeks of class. I also require them to say their name when they contribute to class discussions. Greeting students at the door as they walk in is excellent practice for name recognition in addition to relationship development!

Although I do not assign seats, it seems that students typically sit in the same desks all semester. This helps as well, because I try to go down the rows mentally and repeat their names in my head. Why do I bother? Because I want them to know that I know their names. This isn't a "teacher thing" – this is a human thing. "All human beings are born with a biological need to relate to others" (Diamond & Hopson, 1998).

Granted, the largest class I've taught has been seventy-five students. I would never suggest that professors need to learn every name in a 300-seat lecture hall. I imagine, however, that students would notice and appreciate the effort, nonetheless.

Pedagogically-Related Strategies

Describe the Course and Expectations Early and Often

Research shows that when professors actually describe the structure and purpose of the course, students become more engaged because they know what to expect. "When students understand how and why a particular skill is relevant, they are better prepared to recognize structural similarities in other contexts which may look different on the surface, but in which the same knowledge applies" (Cook and Klipfel, 2015).

When we describe the reason behind the lessons and activities in our courses, it's considered "transparent teaching." We are letting them "behind the curtain," so to speak, which leads to authenticity on our part. "Transparent teaching involves making the implicit explicit for students so they understand why they are engaged in the tasks and what role the course plays in their learning journey" (Jankowski, 2016).

This includes descriptions of class activities as well. Imagine that one of your students texts a friend in your class, asking "Why are we doing this?" You want your students to always have an answer to that question. If your students understand the structure and purpose of each activity, research shows they will be more engaged. "Task value focuses on the student's interest in the subject and beliefs about its importance and usefulness" (McMillan, 2010).

Sometimes I will mix it up and ask students after I have shown them a particular clip or we've finished a certain activity. "Why did we just do that?" or "Why did I show this?" is not only an excellent discussion prompt but it lets them see that there is a "method to my madness" when it comes to keeping them engaged.

Describing the course activities and your expectations are effective techniques to engage your students. You need them to understand the "why" of why you do things, because research shows that, "Students may hold different core beliefs about the nature of intelligence, viewing it as either a fixed entity or as flexible and able to increase. Dependent on these beliefs, students will either recognize the value in making an effort or see effort as fruitless" (Elwick, 2014).

Think of it this way: have you ever been in a meeting where no agenda was given? It's difficult to be fully engaged when one does not know what's coming or what is expected.

 Making your expectations clear – although it sounds simple – can have an impact on student motivation and engagement. McMillan writes that: "Students who believe they are capable engage in more metacognition, use more cognitive strategies, and are more likely to persist at a task" (2010).

She goes further, saying "Effective learning is supported by a motivational component. This aspect might be understood as the 'why' of learning - what gets the student to engage with the learning activity in a way that makes learning possible" (McMillan, 2010).

Encouragement affects more than just engagement. When students believe that their intelligence and achievement levels are not static, effort increases. "Students may hold different core beliefs about the nature of intelligence, viewing it as either a fixed entity or as flexible and able to increase. Dependent on these beliefs, students will either recognize the value in making an effort or see effort as fruitless" (Elwick, 2014).

Clearly describing activities and expectations make you transparent and authentic as an educator. As Jankowski discovered, those expectations lead to engagement. "Students need clear goals in order to understand their progress and to maintain motivation to stay engaged to reach intended goals" (2016).

Discussion Prompts & Problem Solving

We've all been there: the early-morning class where it seems as if the students are still asleep. Trying to have a class discussion under these conditions is daunting for even the most talented professors. There are solutions! "If people are more inherently more likely to be interested in problems than a straight delivery of content, then it follows that organizing lessons around specific problems that relate to the assignment at hand can lead students to be more invested in what they are learning and to thus improve their retention of material" (Cook and Klipfel, 2015).

There is one day in my "Introduction to Mass Media" course where we learn about the music industry. In the past, I have stood in front of the class and described the challenges currently facing that industry. This semester, I tried something a bit different.

I had the students put themselves in small groups and listed the current challenges on the classroom screens. Then I told them to "solve these problems." Instead of listening to me explain the challenges, they were solving them. Instead of merely sitting, they were thinking creatively and cooperatively. The room was loud! Once we came back together as a large group to share their solutions, I discovered that they had identified issues facing the industry that were not even on my radar or in the textbook. We *all* learned something that day, and the experience was student-centered.

Research shows that this type of environment works for our students. "Student-centered, discussion-based and group-based learning activities promote enhanced student participation and interaction and more willingness by students to express their ideas" (Crosling, Heagney and Thomas, 2009).

What challenges are facing your industry or topic of expertise that your students might be able to solve? In what ways can you incorporate those problem-solving skills into your classes?

Avoid The PowerPoint Trap

It's the definition of irony that when I do classroom engagement workshops about how professors need to move past PowerPoint, I use PowerPoint. The truth is that PowerPoint is the default tool for many. "At present, there are an estimated 300 million PowerPoint users (30 million presentations per day) worldwide, give or take five professors on sabbatical" (Berk, 2011).

PowerPoint is not the enemy here. Reading text-filled slides to students is. Yet many of my students tell me that this is the standard routine in many of their classes. When you are developing a new course or lesson, is creation of the slides the first priority for you? Rethink that knee-jerk reaction and try something new.

If you must use slides, remember these "rules." Slides can serve as excellent launching points or outlines for student-centered, active learning activities in your classroom. I challenge you, however, to avoid the standard boring slide and get creative. "You may already

"Slides can be interesting depending on how they're done. I don't mind following them along as long as they are done well." – Chloe Morgan

have slides with bright, saturated colors, flashy templates, and/or dynamite visuals. That's great, but there are still words on most of your slides. So what are your words doing? If they're still cadaver-like text on a screen, you will immediately shift your students into snooze mode from boring to snoring" (Berk, 2011).

It is easier than ever to include animations, GIFs or video into your slides. Features are always being added to PowerPoint, Keynote or Google Slides. Spend some time exploring ways to make your slides active and your students will appreciate the effort!

Questioning Techniques

If your classes are like mine, when you ask the class "Who has questions?" there isn't much of a response. In huge lecture halls, students are less likely to ask questions in front of their peers. After I attended a conference session with Chicago-area instructor and questioning expert Kim Darche, I changed my approach with great results. Instead of "Who has questions?" I now ask "What questions do you have?" This changes the tone. No longer do students have to be embarrassed asking questions, I've already announced that I know questions exist. Kim Darche takes it one step further. She tells her classes "We aren't moving on to the next topic until at least three questions have been answered."

It's also important to ask questions throughout a class period. "When trying to get students to store course information, college instructors must make sure they are paying attention by asking questions throughout the class time" (Lei, Donoso, Foutz, Lasorsa and Oliver, 2011).

 **"I like doing different things in class because it keeps things interesting instead of stale. I hate it when profs read slides to me because I could read the book and get the same information." – Carson Crow**

"When a professor uses nothing but slides, I feel instantly bored. They've become such a normal thing, it's terrible. You already know on your way to classes how they'll go…who wants to show up for that?" – Brie Gurl

Don't think that questioning throughout a class needs to have the feel of constant quizzing. What you're doing is engaging them, encouraging thought. "High quality classroom talk requires the loosening up of the tutor's control and breaking out of the limitations of …recitation" (Hardman, 2016). Questioning – and questioning in the right way – reminds students that they are part of the experience and not merely receptacles of knowledge.

In what ways can you use creative questions to stimulate discussion and thinking in your classes?

Creating Experiences

Dave Burgess, author of *Teach Like a Pirate*, claims that students don't remember lessons as well as they remember experiences. He challenges teachers to create memorable experiences for their students. How does he do it as a high school social studies teacher? During their unit on the 1920s, he hosts a speakeasy complete with a password required to enter the classroom "nightclub." When learning about Henry "Box" Brown, the slave who arranged to have himself mailed to abolitionists in 1849, he has his students try to fit themselves into a box the same size Brown used.

Missouri teacher Matt Hoeckelman dresses as a knight when he teaches about the Middle Ages. When teaching about the coordinate plane, Illinois math teacher Mary Kienstra removes all the furniture from the room and then places an "X" and "Y" axis on the floor with tape. She then gives each student an "address" for them to live on the coordinate plane.

Non-Tech Engagement Strategies

When we talk about the magazine industry in my media class, I prepare by going to the library and getting 75 different magazines which I then place in brown paper bags marked "DO NOT PEEK." What do the students instinctively want to do? Peek! After I have them evaluate the ad on the back of their magazine to predict the target market of that particular publication, I ask them to call the magazine and find out the advertising rates. Right there in class. With their phones.

This past semester, a student left class that day saying: "That was one of the weirdest things I've ever had to do in a class. But that was pretty cool." She will always remember magazine day.

Research shows that Burgess is correct about students remembering specific, unusual classroom experiences. "Instructors must capture students' attention and interest. Novel or surprise events, experiences that have a strong emotional impact, and/or changes in pace of an activity can all be used to capture the attention and interest of students" (Lei, Donoso, Foutz, Lasorsa and Oliver, 2011).

In what way can you provide unique, unforgettable experiences for your students in your classes?

Flipping the Classroom/Avoiding "Info Dump"

Flipping the classroom is the concept of moving lectures and lessons to the online environment which opens up class time for more creative activities. I flipped my classes two years ago. How did I do it? I put my lectures on YouTube and then linked the students to those lectures via links and QR codes on the syllabus.

There are three significant advantages to flipping the college classroom. Students have access to the course material at their own leisure and can stop, pause and rewind the material as needed. Stu-

**"If I'm moving around, it actually helps me remember the material and makes coming to class fun."
– Tiffany Buschman**

dents no longer have the excuse "I missed class that day" because the material is available to them online. Most importantly, flipping the lectures to an online environment provides classroom time for more engaging activities.

 Research has shown that "information dumps" in classrooms do not benefit student retention. Flipping the classroom spreads out the "dumping" and is a way to remind students that learning can take place outside of the classroom, as well. "By limiting the amount of content delivered in a single classroom session, instructors can improve the amount of information that students retain" (Cook and Klipfel, 2015).

Filming videos for my flipped classroom required extra time and planning. Don't tell my secret, but I changed my shirts during the days to make it look like I wasn't filming videos all at once. The reward of that extra work is that my students can use those videos not only for information, but for exam review.

Students' ability to use the videos for their own use at their own convenience is significant. They consume information on their own schedule and at their own pace. Research shows that, "When people are confronted with too much information to process, they turn to a variety of coping behaviors to limit information input" (Rudd and Rudd, 1986).

Don't feel like you need to flip 100 percent of your course materials all at once. Try it with a few of your lectures or lessons and make note of how much extra class time you have for activities that increase your students' engagement.

Movement For Discussion

The last thing many college students want to do – especially at 8 a.m. on a Monday morning – is get up and move around. Yet, research tells us that this movement helps with retention and engagement. "When we move our body and our blood starts pumping... our brain is enjoying and reaping the benefits of rejuvenating blood flow. This increased blood flow physically alters that brain, bathing it in a cascade of growth factors…that create stronger neural connections" (Pasinski and Gould 2011).

So how do we get them out of their seats? There are plenty of opportunities. I have put a "no" poster on one end of the room and a "yes" poster at the other, and when I ask a question they have to answer by moving to the corresponding end of the room. You can name the corners of the classroom A, B, C and D and then ask them multiple choice questions. Think of the introverts in your classroom and how they would appreciate being "heard" without having to use their voices!

Oversized sticky notes or posters are other great tools to encourage student movement. Placing them on the walls and having students or groups of students work on questions or solve equations provides group work, collaboration as well as movement.

I did this once with posters and student groups when we talked about different communication theories. The students described the theory they had been assigned and drew diagrams for emphasis. Although my students were out of their seats and working together, for a moment I panicked because I wasn't sure how the students would take notes on all the theories in the room. Then I saw a student walk around the room taking photos of each poster with her phone. Problem solved!

"Active classes are the best – for sure! Especially when it's a morning class, we all need the extra "umph"" – Makenzi Summers

The lesson here? That my students would surprise me with their ingenuity when given the opportunity. Yours will too.

Formative Assessment

Research tells us that frequent formative assessment can contribute to student engagement and retention. Formative assessment, however, doesn't have to be formal. It can be as simple as having review questions or exercises at the end of class. The point is to make it frequent. "To counteract the effects of decay, college instructors should advise students to frequently review the important course material. They must encourage their students to repeat what they have learned by asking questions for immediate feedback" (Lei, Donoso, Foutz, Lasorsa and Oliver, 2011).

Frequent review keeps students on their toes. "Multiple practice exercises and homework assignments should also be given before an exam for students to practice retrieving information repeatedly" Lei, Donoso, Foutz, Lasorsa and Oliver, 2011). Your learning management system most likely has a quiz option where you can provide practice quizzes for your students.

Want to make it even more engaging? At the end of each class period, ask the students to create some test questions based on what you covered that day. You'll be increasing student engagement, student voice and having them help you with your work simultaneously!

Moving the Furniture

Park and Choi write that "Educational spaces convey an image of educational philosophy about teaching and learning. A standard lecture hall, with immovable chairs all facing the lectern, may represent an educational philosophy of essentialism, which focuses more on "injecting content into students' brains" (Park and Choi, 2014). Yet think of the rooms where you teach. Does the architecture of these rooms represent an effective, engaging educational philosophy?

This is a challenge for many university campuses. One of the rooms where I teach, for example, is a lecture hall with stadium seating and chairs are anchored to the floor. Research says this is just

"To help me remember material, an instructor should repeat important information throughout the lesson. Don't just wait until the end. I need to hear it more than once."
– Jessica Lloyd

about the least effective classroom design for student engagement. "Higher education institutions should pay more attention to the educational impact that classroom design has on students" (Park and Choi, 2014).

Are there ways you can move the furniture in your classroom? It doesn't have to require architectural changes – it can be as easy as moving the desks around. This simple activity can change the chemistry of the room. Students who normally sit in the back might be encouraged to try a new classroom address. The idea is to stir things up and keep students on their toes. Increased engagement is a bonus. "By creating an academic atmosphere in which each space is like the middle of the classroom, students become more interested, motivated, and involved in the learning experience" (Park and Choi, 2014).

The Power of a Story

Are you a good storyteller? Good storytelling can increase your student engagement. "In the college classroom, instructors who tell stories to students in order to convey key pieces of information and content rather than relying on traditional lectures may find that the use of such narratives increases students' interest and memory recall" (Cook and Klipfel, 2015).

Perhaps someone important in your field has a compelling story. Share that with your students. What interesting experiences have you had in your area of expertise? Tell them. "Psychological research has shown that the human memory accords a special place to information in the form of a story" (Cook and Klipfel, 2015).

When we talk about the publishing industry in my "Introduction to Mass Media" course, I tell them the story of my student Nathaniel Giest. On the first day of class, he told me his name was actually "Danger." I nearly snickered because this particular student was about five feet tall and maybe a hundred pounds soaking wet.

Danger never missed a class, never said a word. Until publishing day. He approached me after class and asked if I had any contacts in the publishing industry. (I worked for a book wholesaler when I was in graduate school.) He asked "Would you be willing to read

> **"I remember stories about the information more than I remember the actual information. That sounds weird but it's true." – Kristina Leahy**

the diary that I kept the two years I was in Afghanistan?"

Of course I was willing. He delivered two-hundred loose leaf pages to me the following day and I read his diary. It was phenomenal. He set up a Kickstarter campaign to pay for a cover design and within a few months he had found a publisher.

I tell my students this story because I don't want them to be intimidated by the idea of getting published. Danger did it! Without fail, Danger's story gets mentioned in many of the reflection papers that I have them complete at the end of the term. Students remember stories much more than they remember facts.

What memorable stories can you tell your students?

Small Group Activities

Huge lecture halls aren't conducive to engagement, so a great trick to wake up your students is to give them small group activities. The activities can be discussion questions, problems to solve or issues to research. The point is to break up the large class into smaller groups. Research shows that "Teachers who incorporate small-group activities found increased learning, much greater conceptual understanding, more complex critical-thinking skills, better class attendance and greater confidence" (Cooper, MacGregor, Smith and Robinson 2000).

Small group activities in your classes do more than just increase engagement. Doyle (2008) listed nine benefits of students working with others: (1) improves students intellectually, (2) stimulates interest in learning, (3) increases confidence in intellectual and social abilities, (4) improves understanding of group dynamics, (5) helps students learn to express feelings, (6) helps build assertiveness skills, (7) enhances awareness of diverse views and ideas, (8) exposes students to different ways of thinking, and (9) validates existing ideas and beliefs.

I have found that small group activities in class stimulate conversations and relationships between students who may not have otherwise spoken to each other. These classroom relationships can be connections that lead to increased attendance and success. What's more, they place the focus away from the instructor and onto the students. They learn from each other.

Putting the students in groups doesn't have to be a complicated experience. Sometimes I hand them a playing card as they walk into the room and then have them group themselves based on number or suit on the card. You can have them group themselves by birthday months or the last digit of their phone number. There are apps you can use to break classes into groups, or you can even have them verbally count off. How you get them into groups isn't important. What's important is giving students the opportunity

"Active classrooms are great because everyone is required to participate and work together. This helps us work on team building skills and intercultural communication. Getting out of my seat helps me to really focus on what I'm doing in a world where we are used to sitting like drones." – Merissa Voyles

to try something new in your classroom other than listening to a lecture or reading slides.

Think, Pair and Share

Consider "Think, Pair and Share" as the smallest of the small group activities since it typically only involves two students. In this case, the instructor poses a question or problem and then students think about it, pair off and share what they discover. This might sound simplistic, but research proves otherwise. "Students working in small groups tend to learn more of what is taught and retain it longer than when the same content is presented in other instructional formats" (Davis, 1993).

One of the benefits of this activity is that it engages the introverted student. It enables small-group discussion, which in a large class of 300 can be a plus even for the most extroverted student. When the time allotted has elapsed, ask the students what was discussed. You're not necessarily looking for exact answers here, you're looking for interested, engaged students. The "Think Pair and Share" activity warms them up for larger-group discussions.

This is another activity where student interaction can exist where it might not have otherwise. I've had students tell me they learned so much from a fellow student they had never even noticed before. Research shows that this is beneficial: "Students benefit from collaborative learning situations, where learning is active and interactive between students and their peers" (Crosling, Heagney and Thomas, 2009).

Project Based Learning

Project based learning, or PBL, is the polar opposite of the lecture format. PBL involves students working on a specific project or problem for an extended period of time. In project based learning, lectures are replaced with students analyzing, critiquing and evaluating a particular real-world problem or challenge. Their research and findings typically result in some sort of public product, perhaps a website, speech or magazine.

It is best described by Heather Wolpert-Gawron on the website Edutopia. She explains that "It isn't about building a replica of the Washington Monument. It's about researching someone to honor, designing your own monument, and persuasively pitching a committee to build it" (Wolpert-Gawron, 2015).

She follows by saying that "PBL does not replace your content. It asks that you create a vehicle in which to communicate your content" (Wolpert-Gawron, 2015). The long-term benefits of this approach are clear, especially since many jobs in today's world require problem-solving and research skills. "Project-based work not only increases students' motivation and engagement, it positions them to become strong, successful leaders in a rapidly changing world" (Ball, 2016).

There are many websites with suggestions on how to implement PBL in a higher ed environment. They almost all include the following aspects of PBL: a driving question that leads the project, inquiry and innovation, feedback and revision, reflection and some sort of public presentation of the findings. What you're doing with PBL is giving students autonomy to research and discover something of their choosing that may have real-world implications.

What challenges or problems are facing your industry that your students could analyze through PBL?

 "To help me remember material, teachers should make the students have some sort of vested interest in a project that's more than just a little presentation." – Brooke Zeller

Sketchnoting

Remember how we were taught to take notes? In a linear, outline fashion. Doodling in the margins of notes was seen as a sign of daydreaming or lack of concentration on the material. Current research tells us that is not necessarily the case, and that linear note-taking might not work for everyone. "While doodling has often been seen as frivolous at best and distracting at worst, the idea of sketchnoting has grounding in neuroscience research about how to improve memory. When ideas and related concepts can be encapsulated in an image, the brain remembers the information associated with that image" (Schwartz, 2017).

Sketchnoting is exactly how it sounds: notes taken in sketches, drawings and images rather than words in outline form. It may sound frivolous, but researchers who have tested sketchnoting have discovered that "Drawing enhances memory relative to writing, across settings, instructions, and alternate encoding strategies, both within- and between-participants, visual imagery, or picture superiority" (Wammes, Meade and Fernandes, 2016).

Students don't need to be art majors to be successful at sketchnoting. An effective sketchnote has simple drawings with arrows linking ideas and concepts. However, that doesn't mean that sketchnoting is right for every student. I've had students experience great success with it, and I've had others who are more comfortable with traditional style note-taking.

If you have any students who are particularly non-linear thinkers, encourage them to explore sketchnoting tutorials online. You'll show yourself to be a creative, supportive instructor and they might just become note-taking rock stars with this new approach.

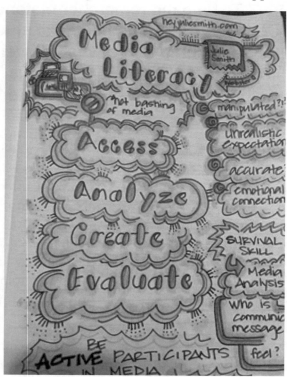

Sketchnote by Anne Reed, used with permission

Take Breaks!

Anyone who has ever taught or taken a four-hour night class knows they can be brutal. Even 90-minute daytime courses can seem to drag. What's the cure for this? Taking breaks. Breaks not only help physically and emotionally, but can prove to be beneficial mentally as well. "Any pleasurable activity used as a brief break can give the amygdala a chance to cool down and the neurotransmitters to rebuild." (Willis, 2007).

 No student can be engaged if material is thrown at them for an extended period of time. In fact, our brains actually form defense mechanisms when we are confronted with too much information. In a college classroom, those defense mechanisms might look like boredom, sleep or cell phones. Give the brains a break! "Learning is not going to be very productive if your brain is suffering from fatigue or angst. It needs rest to prepare itself for more work" (Stormon-Flynn, 2011).

Breaks don't have to be long. They can be thirty seconds or ten minutes. The point to remember is that research shows the brains for our students will work better if we give them time to recharge.

Make an Exit (Slip)

Our K-12 colleagues know all about "exit slips," but most of my professor friends are unfamiliar with this tool. Exit slips describe any activity that a teacher includes near the end of a class or lesson where the students demonstrate what they learned. In some cases, an exit slip might be an actual slip of paper where a student will write their takeaway from that day's class.

Why is the concept of the exit slip important? Research shows that when students reflect on their learning and respond accordingly, retention is increased. Instead of merely dismissing students when your class is over, try an exit slip-type activity. The ways to do this are as varied as the courses we all teach!

An "exit slip" of a lesson can have the recency effect – which is the idea that when people are asked to repeat items in a list, those that come at the end of the list tend to be recalled more than others (*Collins English Dictionary*, 2014). Think of an exit slip as an exclamation point on that day's lesson. You can use it to identify misunderstandings or emphasize key points. Students can use it to summarize or review.

A favorite activity is the "snowstorm," where students write one thing they learned from the day's lesson and then wad up the paper. When prompted, all students throw their paper in the air and then pick up a random "snowball" and share what it says. You can also ask students "If today's class was a movie/book/song, what would its title be?"

Ask students to turn that day's class into an "elevator pitch," where they have 20 seconds to describe the key points of the day. You can have students put their names on index cards and then as they leave the room, have them put their cards into files or piles marked "got it," "more practice please" or even "I have questions."

These are non-techy ways to evaluate student learning at the end of a class. Ways using technology will be discussed in the next chapter. The point is to end class with a bang, not a whimper. Give them something they'll remember as they walk out your door.

CHAPTER 4
ATTITUDES THAT INCREASE ENGAGEMENT

An engaging classroom environment doesn't necessarily mean there are exhilarating experiences happening every single minute. Student engagement can also come from subtle attitudes of you the instructor.

Authenticity

What does it mean to be an authentic instructor? Essentially it means that we are the same inside the classroom as we are outside of it. We let our students see our human side. Perhaps we talk about hobbies or our families. We admit our mistakes and misconceptions. We allow our students to see us as human. What difference does that make?

 Student relationships and engagement are a natural result of instructor authenticity. Authenticity makes us accessible, relatable and approachable. That doesn't mean that students need to know everything about you, we all have our boundaries. However, the research shows that authenticity and accessibility are important since "Students said they were more willing to work with a professor than to work for a professor" (Dunneback and Therrell, 2015). Seeing us as human rather than professor-bots changes the classroom experience for them.

Communications expert Danny Kambel says that authenticity is "found in accountability and responsibility" (Kambel, 2017). Angelo State University instructor Art LaFlamme defines authenticity as 1) bringing in real world examples and experiences and 2) taking the lessons and materials and directly connecting them to what they see around them. Through examples and evidence, abstract concepts aren't [abstract] anymore (LaFlamme, 2017).

LaFlamme goes one step further: "Every instructor should be able to hand their *CV* to their students. Here is my basis for instructing you, and not have a student flinch. It's not salesmanship, it's basis of expertise. Students do not want an instructor who is, so to speak, back on their heels but one who is forward on their toes, working hard to support their learning. Every moment, every day" (LaFlamme, 2017).

Missouri Baptist University professor Suzanne Bright echoes LaFlamme when she says that to be authentic she shares "My own experiences in the classroom, in school leadership, and in my work in professional development. I share both my successes and my failures and how I responded to both, so that students see the value in being reflective and continuing to learn and grow throughout your career" (Bright, 2017).

Students are savvy when it comes to recognizing authenticity. Being authentic is one way to engage them regardless of your technology expertise or subject area.

Enthusiasm

There is no substitute for enthusiasm when it comes to engaging students in the classroom. If you are bored, THEY are bored. Research shows they actually learn less when a professor is not enthused. "Students may not be motivated to learn when faculty deliver course content in a low-key, matter-of-fact way, essentially devoid of overt acts of caring" (Dunneback and Therrell, 2015).

There may be parts of your course that are more interesting to you than others. How does this affect your performance as an instructor? It shouldn't. Even if you're not enthused about the day's particular topic, you can still show enthusiasm for teaching. "Research also distinguishes and indicates that enthusiasm for teaching, rather than enthusiasm for the subject matter, may be more important to student motivation" (Kunter, Tsai, Klusmann, Brunner, Krauss and Baumert, 2008).

In other words, fake it. In a keynote address in June of 2017, education consultant Todd Whittaker said "You don't have to love your job. You just have to ACT like you love your job" (Whittaker, 2017). Why? "Enthusiasm is contagious. You're showing some of yours for the subject matter and the opportunity to teach it will motivate your students' interest in learning it" (Nilson, 2003).

The research does not stop there. "Students may become more willing and better able to learn from a teacher who shows enthusiasm. Four of five students said that enthusiastic teachers cause them to really pay attention and learn in class" (Dunneback and Therrell, 2015).

When an instructor shows enthusiasm, s/he not only shows interest in the topic and in teaching, but the instructor is demonstrating effort to the students. Students notice this. "Students said that hand gestures, body language, tone of voice, pace, facial expressions and upbeat attitude were ways that instructors could display enthusiasm. Students were also attracted to enthusiasm because they respected people who put greater effort into their work" (Dunneback and Therrell, 2015). If we want our students to put greater effort into their work, we can model that behavior for them by being enthusiastic in our classes.

This doesn't mean you need to learn to juggle, tap dance or drink five espressos before every class period. It does mean, however, that your enthusiasm and energy level within the classroom is something that you should note and recognize how it affects engagement within your classroom. "How the material is presented by the instructor is at least as important as whether the material is deemed inherently interesting by students. The presentation of material matters" (Cook and Klipfel, 2015).

 **"I think the energy of the person teaching matters. When a teacher makes us do an activity but has no energy, the students have no enthusiasm and it is boring. When the teacher is excited and tries to make it fun, I am more interested in working hard." – Carson Crow**

> "How can professors help me remember material? Break up the monotony." – Elliott Hawkin

Fearlessness

Many of the ideas and suggestions within this book require risk-taking and change. Those are two things that can typically cause fear. I am here to tell you that fear is a roadblock to truly engaging classrooms. The goal here is not to avoid the change and therefore avoid the fear. The goal here is to be fearless and try a few new things. "Ultimately, effective teaching is fearless" (Christenbury, 2010).

You will never have two identical students or two identical classes. Why assume that what worked with one will automatically work with another? As instructors, we have learned to "teach on the fly" and adapt to all situations. We need to take that one step further and adapt to the ways our students are learning in the 21st Century and make appropriate changes, even if they cause us fear.

Yes, change can be scary. Education expert George Couros writes that "Change can be hard and sometimes seemingly insurmountable, but remember, change is an opportunity to do something amazing" (Couros, 2015). Educators committed to increasing classroom engagement will not fear change, but embrace it.

Fearlessness is not recklessness. It's the willingness to try new things.

Do new things always work out? Not necessarily. Even those situations can be learning experiences, however. Showing your students how have a "Plan B" in place or even how to "go with the flow" can be a worthwhile lesson for them as well. Trust me, they will appreciate the effort.

Fearlessness is more necessary for good teaching than you might think. In fact, in a 1989 study, Boag found fifteen traits that make an effective teacher. Risk taking was one of them (Boag, 1989).

> ## "College instructors should not be afraid to try something new."
> ## – Brie Gurl

Student Choice and Voice

Most college classrooms are not democracies. In fact, I'd say most are monarchies! The movement toward student voice and choice, however, is a strong one. When we encourage choices and voices beyond our own in the classroom, student engagement soars. If students believe they have a say in what happens during their educational experiences, they are more likely to buy into that experience. Researchers agree.

Note what seventeen-year-old Katie Simonds says in her 2015 TEDx talk: "Look at our education system; as students, we have no say on what we learn or how we learn it, yet we're expected to absorb it all, take it all in, and be able to run the world someday" (Simonds, 2015).

Does this mean we instructors give up our authority in the classroom? No. It means we make a point to include our students in the process as much as possible.

"I believe in democratic education—an education in which students have a powerful voice in deciding what they learn, the manner in which they learn, and the manner in which they are held accountable for that learning. I believe that this sort of education is more meaningful for students on many different levels" (Morrison, 2009).

Some colleagues have let their students set the schedule of their course on the syllabus. I put flexible days in my syllabus so that we can discuss what they want to discuss on those particular days. I realize that not every instructor has that flexibility. There are smaller ways to provide for student choice, however.

When I give an assignment, I give them options. Instead of telling them all to write a paper on a particular topic, I suggest a podcast.

Or an online poster. Or a website. Or a cartoon. Or a video. Some students still choose to write a paper, and that is fine. The point is that they have choices that can reflect their interests and personalities. I still grade for content and thoroughness, but now they have different options in which to demonstrate their knowledge.

From a selfish point of view, it's much more fun for me as well. Instead of grading 75 papers, I have a wider, more interesting variety of material to assess. Think of it this way: do you want to assign recipes, or assign something that will reflect student choices? Setting up assignments this way encourages students to be creative and when they have a say in what they create, they will put more effort into the assignment. In other words, "Student voice and their preferences matter" (Dunneback and Therrell, 2015).

Student voice is a harder nut to crack. We all have Hermoine Grangers who are anxious to answer every question, but what about the introverts in the class who might not be as willing to share their voice? With research telling us that student voice in the classroom is so important, we need to reflect on ways we can incorporate the voices of the nearly fifty percent of our students who classify themselves as introverts.

My oldest son is currently an engineering major who gets frustrated when professors in his elective courses penalize him for not participating in class. He understands that classroom participation is important, but struggles with the perception that if he's not communicating with his voice, that he's not engaged in class. "I'm a thinker, Mom – not a talker." What's the solution?

There are technological ways that introverts can insert their student voice into class, but there are non-tech ways as well. Since introverts typically require a bit more time to formulate a response, instructors should make sure to provide that time in class. Media scholar Paige Turner suggests that instructors tell students to write down their responses on paper before she calls on a student. That way, everyone has a chance to prepare and introverts know they may be called upon.

I've gone "old school" before and handed out red and green cardstock to my students for voting purposes. It's much easier for some students to "use their voice" by holding up a red or green card rather than speak in front of an auditorium with 75 students.

There will always be the students who have no trouble answering every single question in class. The key is to engage ALL students and make them feel like their voices matter. Give them as many choices in the classroom as possible, and encourage student voice at every opportunity. The result will be a fully engaged, enthusiastic classroom where each student feels that they have value. We owe it to them. "Every instructor owes it to students to assess their perceptions of learning activities and then modify teaching accordingly" (Lumpkin, Achen and Dodd, 2015).

Innovation Mindset

Innovation is quite the buzzword in education today. What does it mean, exactly? It means instead of seeing roadblocks, you see opportunities. It means that you are constantly looking at situations from various angles and trying to improve them. You are solutions-driven and resourceful.

The opposite of an innovation mindset is the closed mindset. The closed mindset is the colleague who says "We've always done it that way." The administrator who says "That can't be done". The teacher who says "I'm just not creative". These are mental roadblocks. They are dangerous, and they are contagious.

Teaching itself is an innovative act. None of us repeatedly teach the exact same material to the exact same students, we are responding to dozens of variables every time we walk into a classroom. Education author Perc Marland explains: "What teaching effectiveness is, varies according to time, place and the learners in the classroom. What is effective for one teacher will not work for another teacher. What is effective in Grade 1 will certainly not be effective in Grade 6 or Grade 12. What is effective in this era will not be effective in the next. Teaching effectiveness varies from teacher to teacher, class to class and from one era to the next" (Marland, 2007).

George Couros takes it one step further and writes that innovative teachers also are empathetic teachers: they think about the classroom environment and learning opportunities from the point of view of the student, not the teacher (Couros, 2015). He asks a very basic question: "Would you want to be a learner in your own classroom?"

If you answered that question negatively, it is time for you to reflect on your own mindsets and how they affect engagement within your classroom.

Having an innovation mindset is good modeling for the students as well, since much has been written about how our students need to be innovative themselves. When Thomas Friedman wrote about Google's hiring practices, he summarized by saying "The world only cares about — and pays off on — what you can do with what you know" (Friedman, 2014).

Students – like excellent teachers – need to learn on the fly. We can model that for them with an innovation mindset. "The key to teaching creativity and innovation skills lies in creating quality learning environments that give learners the opportunity to solve authentic, real-world problems and to be inquisitive with an open mind" (Kivunja, 2014). In an innovative environment, engagement will take root!

Don't Take Yourself Too Seriously

The last engagement-centered attitude is simply this: don't take yourself too seriously in the classroom. There's no rule that says fun and learning need to be mutually exclusive! The research bears this out: "Fun delivery was demonstrated to have a positive relationship with engagement. Fun delivery exhibited the strongest effect with emotional engagement, followed by cognitive engagement and physical engagement. Accordingly, fun delivery appears to most strongly influence affective reactions and to a lesser degree whether students' minds are focused and whether they expend effort in a course" (Tews, Jackson, Ramsay and Michel, 2015). You have nothing to lose. Have some fun.

Student Engagement Strategies for Your Teaching

Educators are being encouraged to place more emphasis on the attention and interest students show in class. Engaged students will be more curious about a subject — perhaps even more passionate about it. Increasing engagement can help to improve student motivation and, in turn, boost student learning, progress and achievement as well as overall learning outcomes.

1. Active learning: Create a teaching and learning environment primed for student participation, such as calling on students to answer a question, individual reflection, think pair share and group problem-solving.

2. Participatory teaching: This student-centered approach to pedagogy accounts for the different skills, backgrounds and learning styles of students. The focus of participatory teaching is on self-regulation and self-reflection; specific strategies include using different teaching methods and varying means of assessment.

3. Flip the classroom: Flip the traditional lecture-homework relationship. Students study the subject matter independently and outside class through tools such as pre-recorded videos. Class is then spent on student-centered learning such as working through problems, debating or group work.

4. Technology in the classroom: Students expect to be constantly connected and want immediate feedback. Online and mobile technology can be used to provide active learning activities and to keep students engaged outside the classroom.

5. Writing: Exercises such as journaling and one-minute papers can help to keep students engaged in class as well as improve thinking skills.

6. Set expectations: At the beginning of a course, ask students what they expect from you and then try to meet those expecta-

tions. Students are more engaged when they have a good relationship with the instructor.

7. Integrated curriculum: Combine disciplines rather than compartmentalizing subjects. Some medical schools, for example, have moved away from teaching subjects in isolation such as physiology and anatomy, and moved toward studying organ systems where students learn the physiology and anatomy associated with that system.

8. Make the course relevant: Students want courses to be relevant and meaningful. Use real-world examples to teach; where the course is relevant to a specific occupation, ensure it is aligned with the current needs of the occupation.

9. Cooperative learning: Arrange students in partners or small groups to help them achieve learning goals. Group work can include assignments, discussions, reviews and lab experiments — even having students discuss a lesson with their peers.

10. Authentic learning experiences: Students tackle real-world problems and attempt to come up with a solution through methods such as inquiry and experimentation. Ideally, the solution will benefit others or the community. Experiential learning—when students learn from reflecting on their real-world learning experience—is a further development of this, and is an effective teaching strategy.

From Tophat.com, used here with permission. https://tophat.com/ blog/student-engagement-strategies/

CHAPTER 5
Engagement Through Technology

So far, we've talked about engagement tools that require no technical knowledge or ability. The wonderful thing about most new tech tools, however, is that they are extremely intuitive and easy, even for the most reluctant, techno-phobic instructor.

If you are afraid of technology, it's time for you to embrace an innovator's mindset and try something new. Don't categorize technology as something that is too difficult or unnecessary for education. Consider technology as something that opens up hundreds of

 "Teachers should interact with the students and do fun stuff. Be loud. Be goofy. Your students will remember everything." – Shane Wheatley

new opportunities for you in the classroom, especially since research tells us that our students welcome it. "The new technologies we now have remove the need for traditional teaching. In addition, we now understand much better how people actually learn. The combination of this understanding with new technologies is resulting in the most revolutionary time in education since the invention of the printing press" (Macknight, 2016). Technology in the classroom is not scary. It is *exciting*!

Think of the information and opportunities available to our students in their back pockets. Students spend so much time out of class creating their own media with all sorts of tech tools – why should that stop in the classroom? If you are sincerely interested in increasing engagement in your classroom, you must embrace the idea that tech is your ally, not your enemy.

Macknight writes: in today's world, are the traditional trappings of the classroom even relevant? "Today, so much of what we used to do in teaching is now unnecessary. Students really don't need textbooks or even conventional lectures anymore" (Macknight, 2016).

If a doctor only used tools available a hundred years ago to operate on someone, we would call that malpractice. Why should our standards for education be lower?

Edtech evangelizer Tony Vincent reminds us that we should not "marry" any particular website, since the industry is fluid. He encourages us to "date" web tools without the commitment. I agree. Most of the sites listed in this chapter are more alike than they are different, many are simply a matter of personal preference. It's up to *you* to play around with them and see which sites you like the best. The point, however, is to play.

The specific resources I have listed in this chapter are web-based tools. There are apps and extensions that might also do the same thing as the tools I have listed, but since apps and extensions have such a fluid existence, I decided to limit my suggestions to websites. If you fall in love with a tech tool in this chapter, there is most likely an easy-to-find corresponding app or web extension.

One more thing: the sites I have listed in this chapter have free versions. If you desire all the bells and whistles, you may have to pay in some cases. I try to use tech engagement tools weekly, and yet there is only one of these websites for which I pay a fee. Don't be discouraged, it's very possible to be engaging and tech-y without spending a dime.

Screencasting

Have you ever had a student who was horrified at the thought of doing a class presentation? Do you have introverts who are more comfortable speaking in front of a screen rather than an auditorium of classmates? Screencasting is a fantastic tool to add to your engagement toolbox.

Screencasting is simply the recording of what's happening on your computer screen, either with or without narration and accompanying video. There are several websites that offer free screencasting, most are more alike than they are different. My personal favorite is www.screencastomatic.com which offers free screencasts up to fifteen minutes each in length. (If you need a cast longer than fifteen minutes, you will need a subscription to the site.)

This website is multi-functional: it can do simple screencasts or it can include narration. If you choose to film yourself while narrating, you can choose where to place your video image on the screen. Another benefit of this particular site is that once the screencast is complete, there are options. Students can upload the video to their YouTube channel, or simply save it on their device.

I have given screencasts as options in assignments, and it's always so interesting to see how students frame and deliver them. Doing screencasts offers them the ability to do several "takes" (unlike a traditional class presentation) and the excellent ones can be preserved in digital portfolios. One student applied for a job using a screencast instead of just emailing a resume!

Screencasts can help your students if you are flipping your classroom. Even if you don't flip, a screencast of a video lecture can help your students with material review. I have had non-native English speaking students tell me that the videos help them because in many cases they are close-captioned.

Research tells us that the "Benefits of screencasting include flexible and personalized learning, enhanced understanding, facilitated exam review, provided multimodal support, helped students make up for missed lectures and stay on track, provided a vicarious learning experience, served as a memory aid, filled in gaps in class notes and made learning fun" (Ahmad, Doheny, Faherty and Harding, 2013).

Screencasting Sites to Explore:

www.screencastomatic.com

www.screentoaster.com

www.free-screencast.com

Online Posters

Remember those days of buying a poster board to make a display or report for school, then running out of room on the right side or the bottom? Those days are over. Online posters make creation simple, multimedia and unlimited for both you and the students.

There are several online poster-making sites that are fairly popular and extremely easy to use. Many feature drag-and-drop options for photos or videos as well as intuitive text editing. Students can change or color backdrops and/or fonts and even include links to sites. These images can then be downloaded, shared or stored. The possibilities here are endless.

Engagement Through Technology

ThingLink.com is also an online poster site where you upload a photo as your background, and then add links via dots on the image. The links can be articles, videos, audio files, or a student's own writing. It's truly an interactive poster. One term in my online course, I had students do ThingLinks where they introduced themselves to the class. It was creative, interactive and much more fun than a standard discussion board icebreaker question.

These online poster platforms can make anyone look like a graphic designer without any graphic design experience – or talent!

Online Poster Sites to Explore:

www.thinglink.com

www.padlet.com

www.canva.com

www.postermywall.com

www.spark.adobe.com

Other Uses for Online Posters

Online poster-making sites have many other uses. If you create a poster on Padlet and share the link, for example, anyone with the link can collaborate on your poster. This can add a whole new dimension to class discussions or group projects.

I have created Padlets before and shared the link with the class. Perhaps the Padlet poses a question. Anyone with the link to the Padlet can respond! So instead of two students monopolizing a class discussion, ALL of my students – even the introverts – have a way to add their voice. You can arrange your Padlet so that student responses are shown chronologically or randomly. Again, it's up to you to play around with the possibilities.

This feature of Padlet makes it ideal for collaborative note-taking, group projects, or even asking students what they remember the most from a previous class. Students can use Padlet as a document hub or a photo album. The possibilities are endless. I encourage you to check out Matt Miller's website, www.ditchthattextbook. com for more ideas on how to use Padlet as well as countless other web creation tools.

www.ditchthattextbook.com

Remind

Have you ever wished you could send out a group text to your students without having to enter (or even know) all of their cell numbers? Especially since college students rarely read email messages, the ability to text them should be in every professor's tech toolbox.

The website www.remind.com is an excellent resource for this exact scenario. Create a "class" on the website and you will be given a code to share with students that they enter via text to a number provided by the site. Once they have done that, their numbers are now on your class list and you can text the class without having to know their numbers and without them knowing yours.

I've used Remind to let students know if I have the flu or if our room assignments have changed. I've also used the site to remind classes about exams. Although students are used to receiving many text messages, I am careful to not inundate them with messages. Short and infrequent are the important words to remember here, but the ability to text them all at once is something I don't want to ever give up.

I do not require my students to sign up for my Remind messages. I do, however, let them know how beneficial it might be to find out about a cancelled class before actually getting there. Students usually appreciate the effort in attempting to reach them.

Want to try something super engaging? Create a Padlet before class and ask a question on the Padlet. Then about ten minutes before class begins, send the link to the Padlet via your Remind class list. Each student will get your link-filled text on their way to class, typically while they are already looking at their phones.

They can click on the link to the Padlet and then answer the question on their way to your class. Before class begins, you have already engaged your students! Remind and Padlet are excellent tools to use together.

Remind also has a mobile app if you need to send a message while you're on the go. You can also set up your classes so that students can respond to one of your Remind texts. I, however, have never exercised that option.

Sites like Remind:

www.remind.com

www.bloomz.net

www.sendhub.com

www.classparrot.com

Mind Mapping

Do you have any students who are non-linear thinkers? Mind mapping is perfect for them. Students can create and use mind maps to represent ideas, notes or concepts. When students create mind maps, you are able to see their train of thought and level of understanding. You can also use mind maps to plan out lessons or lectures. Mind maps stir things up! Similar to sketchnoting, "Mind mapping avoids dull, linear thinking, jogging your creativity and making note taking fun again" (Litemind, 2012).

Mind maps work in the way our brains work: in a radiant way rather than a linear way. Research shows that mind mapping can significantly help long-term memory (Farrand, 2002). Glass and Holyoak claim that mind mapping leads to the "chunking" of information, which improves recall (Glass and Holyoak, 1986).

Mind maps are an excellent tool for creativity as well as memory. Since the space of an online mind map is unlimited, students can visualize and infinite number of thoughts and ideas. These sites are perfect for brainstorming sessions or collaborative projects. Mind maps can help students organize thoughts before they begin writing, or demonstrate visual concepts in a colorful and creative way. Research backs this up. A 2009 study (even before many of these sites were available) concluded that mind mapping improved student's ability to generate, visualize and organize complex ideas (Al-Jarf, 2009).

Many of these mind mapping sites are more alike than they are different, it all depends on which site you and your students prefer. I typically provide one or two options when I assign a mind map and have the students choose. Here are some to play with:

https://www.mindvectorweb.com/

https://www.mindmup.com/

https://www.mindomo.com/

http://chartgizmo.com/

Engagement Through Technology

Cell Phone Specific Tools

What About the Cell Phones?

You might be concerned that many of these engagement tools involve cell phone use in the classroom. We have all fought this battle one way or another – to allow cell phones in class or not. So much of this issue depends on the type of class and its size. It's unreasonable to think that one can prohibit cell phone use in a lecture auditorium that seats three hundred students. It's also unreasonable to think cell phone use is appropriate in a seminar course with ten students. The instructor's relationship with cell phones in class can change depending on the course, the student or the day! With that in mind, I share my attitude about these ubiquitous tools.

My class sizes are typically between 20-40 students. I used to teach in a lecture-hall setting but our building has since been remodeled and I am now in what they call the "Active Learning Lab", where I have tables that each have screens attached. I tell my students at the beginning of the term that I will not take their phones, nor will I ask them to put their phones away. After all, we occasionally use them in class. My attitude will change, however, if I see a student simply sitting in the class, unengaged, while on their phone. Why even come to class? (That's a topic for another book!)

I have a colleague who will count a student absent if he sees them with their phone in his class. I don't begrudge or blame him, but I have a different attitude. If I see a student on their phone, I take that as a sign that I need to "up my game". I've also discovered that if we use phones in class for pedagogical activities, the students are more likely to put them away when we are finished. Perhaps it is the whole "forbidden fruit" idea, I'm not sure. There is enough research on this to keep the debate going.

 There is research showing that students view prohibitive cell phone policies as largely ineffective (Berry and Westfall, 2015). There is also research showing that students in a classroom where cell phones are prohibited tend to view their instructors more favorably, which seems illogical since students love their phones so much (Lancaster, 2018). Frey and Tatum discovered that policies encouraging cell phone use appear to result in greater perceptions of instructor caring, competence, and trustworthiness than discouraging policies (Frey and Tatum, 2016).

In other words, the jury is still out regarding cell phone use. That's why I encourage you to find your own policy, one that works for you, your students and your area of study.

The Cell Phone as Your Pedagogical Partner

Many of my colleagues might consider this next section nothing more than higher education heresy. However, I say it with great pride: "I encourage cell phone use in my classroom."

I will follow this up with specifics, however: I think texting and playing with a phone during class is rude and unacceptable. I also consider it a sign that I need to step up my game and be more engaging.

Cell phone use in the classroom follows the "forbidden fruit" pattern. If we are militant about outlawing their use, some students take that as a direct challenge. Besides, you know that today's college student is touching their phone nearly every moment of every day. If you teach in a large auditorium, you know that policing cell phone use is next to impossible anyway.

By encouraging occasional use of the phone as a pedagogical tool, students are less likely to use them inappropriately. "The greatest barrier to permitting cell phones in the classroom has been teachers' perception that they are disruptive" (Lenhart, 2010).

I challenge you to view the cell phone as your partner in pedagogy rather than your enemy. "The instances of how the cell phones can be used in learning are numerous: from short written assignments, quizzes, surveys, podcasts to blogs, e-books, electronic dictionary, vocabulary games, etc" (Frey and Tatum, 2016).

Just today, I had my students pull their phones out to look up radio station ownership. They kept their phones out for an online quiz that I developed on the history of the radio industry. Far from being disruptive, the phones engaged them. Besides, what college student isn't going to love it when a professor says "Get your phones out!"? The research backs this up.

More than half of the teachers surveyed in a 2011 study stated that cell phone use in their classrooms increased engagement (Thomas, O'Bannon and Bolton 2013).

You can engage your learners on the first day by putting QR codes on your syllabus. Most students have QR code readers on their phones, and all web browsers have QR code creation extensions. If you flip your classroom and have some online lectures, create QR codes of the lectures and put them in the syllabus rather than links that the students would have to type in. The most recent operating systems don't even require a QR code reader app – simply point the camera at a QR code and the phone will take you there.

You can create QR code scavenger hunts around your room or building. You can have students interview each other or experts using the recording features of their phones. They can record your lectures or take photos of slides or notes. You can have them participate in formative assessment. I have even encouraged them to double-check facts and figures I might mention in a lecture via their phones. The list of ways a cell phone can be used in a classroom is only limited by your imagination.

The easiest way to begin cell phone use in your classroom is through online, real-time polling sites. PollEverywhere, for example, has word cloud, survey and open-ended question options. You create the question, share the link with the class, and they "vote" using their phones. Remember the clickers some schools used to have? Think of cell phones as high-tech, updated clickers.

If you have a particular topic in class that you like to discuss which you think might be a bit difficult for students to discuss openly, try a cell phone polling exercise. You'll get honest, anonymous responses.

These sites are also excellent for exam review. If most of the class gets a question incorrect, I know I need to go over the material in a more effective way. You won't have to enter the questions each term, because the sites save the questions for you when you create an account.

www.polleverywhere.com

www.mentimeter.com

https://crowdsignal.com/

https://www.tallyspace.com/

Skype and/or Google Hangout

Have you ever wished that you could have an expert in your field do a guest lecture? I have good news. You can, via Skype or Google Hangout! Reach out to scholars in your field, the author of a textbook or the book your class just finished reading or a scientist doing amazing work. The possibilities are endless.

I've had authors Skype my class on book industry day. I saw an interesting article in the Huffington Post last year by a woman who described spending two hours staging each of her Instagram photos and asked her to Skype my class to answer questions. Chicago-area elementary teacher Mary Kienstra has had shark scientists from OCEARCH Skype her class when they are studying sharks. The director of the documentary "Catfish," Nev Schulman, Skyped my class to answer questions after we viewed his film.

The good news is that experts and authors are usually all-too-willing to talk about themselves – I have yet to be declined. Skyping in class shows students that you are connected and willing to reach out to others. It's engaging for them because it is a different experience! The scheduling can sometimes be a challenge, but it's worth the effort.

Is your brain buzzing with ideas of people who could Skype your classes? It should be.

www.skype.com

https://hangouts.google.com/

www.zoom.com

Presentation Tools That Go Beyond PowerPoint

Irony is when I do a presentation on different engagement strategies and the importance of trying new things – but I use PowerPoint to do the presentation. It's the default presentation tool for most of us. There are other slide tools, but for some the learning curve of a new program is too daunting. I want to challenge you to try it – not just to expand your knowledge, but to impress your students.

Prezi was very popular for a while, but many completed Prezis involved so much movement they nearly induced motion sickness. If one can rein in the temptation to zoom in and out too quickly, a well-organized Prezi can be an excellent presentation tool. It's very easy to embed YouTube videos in a Prezi, and its bracket feature is ideal for chunking similar ideas or materials. If you haven't played with Prezi, ask one of your students. They know it.

Pechakucha is a presentation tool with an interesting hook: it is twenty slides and each slide is shown for twenty seconds. This format requires some editing and planning, for the program moves the slides on a schedule regardless of where you are with your narration. Students who use Pechakucha definitely have to know their material, because they can't stand there and read slides. I have not used Pechakucha for myself in the classroom, but I sure enjoy assigning them. A student who chooses to present a Pechakucha is a well-prepared student!

Many PowerPoint alternatives have stunning visuals and themes. Take a look at www.emaze.com and www.haikudeck.com for compelling images that make PowerPoint themes look downright dull.

If you're less interested in design and more interested in non-linear presentation content, then www.slidebean.com might be for you. This site claims all you do is enter the content and they will design the presentation for you.

www.emaze.com

www.haikudeck.com

www.slidebean.com

Infographics

It seems obvious that we live in a visual culture rather than a literate one. In fact, research tells us that it takes fifty seconds to read 200-250 words but only 1/10 of a second to process a visual scene (Hughes, 2015). Infographics take advantage of this visual ability by presenting vast amounts of data in a sorted, visually-appealing way.

There's much more to infographics than just being attractive, however. "Infographics can be engaging alternative products of research because the multimodal format invites students to make sense of complex information by applying multiple literacies" (Abilock and Williams, 2017). In order to create an infographic, a student must process complex information, curate it and then decide in what visual ways to present it.

I have assigned infographics as options within certain assignments. It's always fascinating to see what the students create! It's also a very easy way to determine which of your students are graphic design majors – their infographics turn out looking professional! Infographics are terrific additions to a student's digital portfolio as well. It should be noted that when a student submits an infographic as an assignment, I am still judging them on the material presented, mechanics and citations. I do not teach design courses, so I don't take that part of the infographic into account. I am merely providing them with a choice of how to present their knowledge – and I still grade for content, if not for visual design.

There are several free websites that are excellent for infographic creation. Take a look and see which ones might work best for your students and then set them loose in this visual playground.

www.piktochart.com

www.visme.com

https://www.canva.com/create/infographics/

www.infogram.com

Podcasting Tools

Thirty-nine percent of college students listen to podcasts monthly. Conversely, 40 percent of Americans have never heard of the medium. A podcast is a digital voice recording on any topic which tells a story or mimics a radio program.

There are podcasts available online about every topic imaginable. I assign podcasts as homework. Students tell me that listening to podcasts for homework is engaging because they can listen while driving, walking or working out. Podcasts are truly "homework on the go." Think about putting your class lectures in podcast format. Research shows that podcasts are beneficial to our students. "A noticeable benefit associated with the use of podcasting as a form of asynchronous learning is the ability to manage personal learning and maximize convenience. Students can access the review sessions at their leisure and are not limited to a single exposure of the review session" (Jalali, Carnegie, Hincke, Sun, Gauthier and Leddy, 2011).

Share your slides with students, and their ability to listen to your lectures in podcast form while viewing slides can be an effective learning strategy for many of your students. "The combination of the auditory podcasts and visual PowerPoint slides permitted the students to process information simultaneously using two different modalities. This maximized their use of working memory and facilitated their learning" (Jalali, Carnegie, Hincke, Sun, Gauthier and Leddy, 2011).

Take podcasts one step further, and ask your students to produce their own podcasts. The key is to give them detailed instructions about the length required and your expectations regarding content and technical requirements.

The first time I assigned a podcast, half of my students were thrilled and half were terrified. I told them that the issue would not be the technical aspects of the podcast, but the content. The preparation, research and delivery were the most important aspects of the assignment, at least for my course. I did have several audio production majors who added fancy sound effects to their podcasts, but that did not affect their grade.

You will notice that when you tell your students how long you expect their podcasts to be, they will think what you're assigning is too long. When the podcasts are due, however, the students will all tell you that they "didn't have enough time." It never fails.

The podcasts are an exciting, engaging way for students to demonstrate their knowledge to you. You will be able to critique their podcasts while on a walk or driving! You sure can't do that when you're grading papers.

Engagement Through Technology

There are many podcast apps available for smart phones. The sites listed below are online podcast creation sites that you should explore. When I assign podcasts, I typically give them several options to choose from and let the students choose which one they want to use.

www.podbean.com

www.podomatic.com

www.spreaker.com

If you're not used to incorporating technology into your courses, these tools might seem intimidating. If you're a bit overwhelmed by the idea of these tech-y engagement tools, remember that you don't have to try all of them. I recommend you choose one or two to integrate and see how your students respond. As your confidence grows, incorporate a few more. I guarantee that you will see student engagement, student creativity and everyone's enthusiasm grow.

CHAPTER 6
Engagement with Tech Assessment Tools

So far, we have talked about using technology to help engage students through creative work. Can we use technology, however, to assess their learning as well? The answer is YES. Gone are the days when you are unaware of your students' progress until you grade the exams. There are so many tools available to professors now that continuous formative assessment is not only easy but pedagogically sound.

I am not advocating the abandonment of traditional classroom discussions or quizzes. What I do support, however, is the use of a variety of tools to measure the progress of every student – whether they be extroverted or introverted – before the quizzes are given.

Google Forms

When I first started teaching, I would hand out a short survey to my students on paper during the initial class period. I asked them standard questions about their hometowns, their interest, etc. Then I would put the sheets in a binder and (most likely) never look at them again.

Three semesters ago, I began to do these questionnaires on Google Forms. I share the link with my students (along with the QR code) and they can fill out the form on their devices while in class. The Google form offered some improvements over the "dead tree" version: when creating the questions I could take advantage of Google's drop-down menu options. Once the students were finished, their entries went straight to my Google Drive in a Google Sheet so I had access to that information all the time, not just when I had my binder handy.

I also experimented with different questions besides the standard "hometown" and "major." The version I gave this semester included the questions "What's one thing you would like me to know about you?" and "What can I do to help you be successful in this class?"

Their responses not only helped me as an instructor, but helped me get to know them as individuals – which, if you teach in a large auditorium like I do – can be next to impossible. I've also had students tell me they appreciated that someone actually asked these questions.

My experience is that students are more willing to submit information electronically than on paper (besides, have you seen student handwriting lately? Terrifying.) My response rate using Google Forms is 50 percent higher than when I handed out paper questionnaires. If you are interested in learning more about your students through technology, I would strongly recommend trying a Google Form. You never know what you might learn!

www.google.com/forms

Kahoot

Kahoot might be my favorite tech engagement tool! It has several uses, but for this chapter we will concentrate on how it can be used for formative assessment. Kahoot is a real-time assessment tool where students answer your pre-written questions with a device and their responses show up on the screen.

A classroom quiz done on Kahoot revolves around questions you write that have four multiple-choice responses. When you open the Kahoot site in class, you click on the particular Kahoot you'd like the class to play, and an access code appears on the screen. The students use their devices to go to www.kahoot.it and then they enter the access code so your game will appear.

The students enter in a name, and when the class is ready, you start the Kahoot. Each question appears on the screen (you can pre-determine the amount of time the question is visible) and then the responses are color coded. To choose the correct response, the student clicks on the corresponding color on their device. They are immediately told by Kahoot if their response is correct.

After each student has answered the question, the standings appear. Then you advance the Kahoot to the next question. When all the questions are completed, a winner is announced. You might think that college students are too sophisticated to play such a "game" in class. I challenge you to try it. I've seen tough athletes sit on the edge of their seats during Kahoots, desperate to win. I've seen high-fives and trash-talking during Kahoots. They get into it.

A Kahoot works very well for exam reviews or at the beginning of a unit to determine students' baseline knowledge of a topic. If many students answer a Kahoot question incorrectly during an exam review, I know that I need to go over that material in a bit more detail. One semester, I challenged my class saying that if they ever answered a Kahoot question 100% correctly, I would do a cartwheel in class. They did, I did the cartwheel, and it ended up on Instagram. Of course.

Kahoot has added a "team" feature which I have yet to try. There are also plenty of Kahoots that have already been created by other instructors that are "public," meaning you can use Kahoots that already exist. I would encourage you to set up a Kahoot account and explore.

www.getkahoot.com

Quizizz

Quizizz is the quieter, more laid-back version of Kahoot. Where Kahoot is loud and has the whole class answering the same questions at the same time, Quizizz is a similar process but involves the students working at their own pace.

You create Quizizz questions in advance and instruct the students to go to www.quizizz.com site and enter the access code given. The students enter a name, and Quizizz will assign them an avatar. Then they may begin answering the questions at their own pace, on their own device.

A classroom working on a Quizizz is a quiet room! One thing students really enjoy about this tool is that the site employs memes which are shown to the kids after each response. If they answer a question correctly, they are congratulated. If they answer incorrectly, the meme mocks them. It may sounds harsh, but our students speak in memes and I have found they enjoy it immensely. The creator of the Quizizz can also upload their own meme examples to deploy, although I have not tried that yet.

My introverted students prefer Quizizz over Kahoot. Kahoot is loud, competitive and rewards extra points for speed. Quizizz is much more laid-back and the speed of response does not matter. You as the instructor still get access to which questions were answered correctly, and that information can be downloaded into a spreadsheet.

www.quizizz.com

EdPuzzle

Have you ever assigned a YouTube video for homework and then wondered if the students actually viewed it? EdPuzzle is the engaging answer to this question!

When you go to the www.edpuzzle.com website, you have the ability to enter the URL of any YouTube video. Then the magic begins.

As the video plays on the EdPuzzle site, you can press pause and then embed your own question within the video. Students are unable to keep watching the video unless they have answered your question. You can embed as many questions within the video as you'd like. Once you are done adding your questions within the video, you have a new link to share with your class.

They watch the video but they must answer your questions in order to complete the video. The student responses are automatically inserted into a Google form. Now you have data showing you which students watched the video and how they responded to your questions!

This makes it a wonderful tool for the introverts in your class as well. They can contribute to the conversation and answer your questions on their own time without having to speak to the entire class.

EdPuzzle is a great way to super-charge your classroom engagement. Explore the site and see in what ways you can utilize it to bring YouTube videos to life for your students!

www.edpuzzle.com

Content Curation

It's no secret that our students have the world of information at their fingertips. There is no challenge for them to find information. The challenge is for them to find information that is meaningful, valid and true. This is where content curation sites can hone their critical thinking skills as well as their engagement.

I have used content curation sites in various ways in my classroom. One semester, I had each student begin the class by presenting a "Livebinder" (www.livebinder.com). Since I teach about the media, the student's assignment was to create a Livebinder with what they considered to be the most important media-related stories of the week. Livebinder is a virtual, online notebook where students can upload material or insert links into binders that they have organized themselves.

The websites PearlTrees (www.pearltrees.com) and Bag the Web (www.bagtheweb.com) are similar to Livebinder but they are organized a bit differently. With PearlTrees, a student creates more of a mind map with links organized in certain "trees." With Bag the Web, the student organizes content and then places it in "bags" that the student has labeled. My male students tend to like Bag the Web the best, although organizing the materials into sub-categories is more difficult.

Using www.paper.li, students can create a virtual newsletter based on search terms or topics and then share across multiple platforms. The idea behind content curation is encouraging the student to evaluate material for authenticity and relevance. If they have a bit of fun doing it in the process, all the better!

"College instructors should not be afraid to try something new."
– Brie Gurl

www.livebinder.com

www.pearltrees.com

www.bagtheweb.com

www.paper.li

Answer Garden

Answer Garden is a minimalistic site created strictly for providing feedback. It's marketed toward conferences and speeches but also works very well within the classroom. Simply create a question at the Answer Garden website (www.answergarden.ch) and share the site with your students. They can provide immediate feedback which shows up on the Answer Garden page. It's very similar to Padlet (www.padlet.com) which we discussed earlier, but it is focused primarily on feedback and doesn't have the multi-media functionality of Padlet.

I use Answer Garden in class to find out how comfortable my students are with the material we just covered, if they're ready to move on to the next topic and/or if they have any questions. The responses can be anonymous, and they can also be put into word clouds. This tool is useful for introverts who might have additional questions but prefer not to ask them in front of the entire class.

www.answergarden.ch

Go SoapBox

Here's a common scenario: you introduce a new concept in class and then ask if anyone has any questions. You are greeted with silence. Ever wish there was a way to determine which students are understanding the material and which students are confused? The site Go SoapBox (www.gosoapbox.com) gives you that option.

Go SoapBox is an interactive student response system that has several interesting features. Students can access features on any device and no app installation is necessary. The site has real-time polling and quiz options. It also has an interesting Q&A feature that enables students to vote on the most popular questions so that these questions rise to the top of the list. You will then be able to answer the most pressing student questions.

Go SoapBox also has a compelling feature called the "Confusion Barometer." When this feature is enabled, the students see a toggle menu at the top of their screen. One button says "I am getting it" and the other says "I'm confused". The teacher view of this screen gives the instructor real-time information regarding the current confusion level of their students. You no longer have to wait until exam time to find out if your students understand the material!

www.gosoapbox.com

Plickers

Tired of asking students to get out a device? Plickers (https://get.plickers.com/) might be the tool for you. Instead of using a device to answer a question, students use a printed out sheet (available at the website) that contains a QR code and hold it one of four ways. When you open the installed Plickers app on your device, you simply aim your device at your class while they hold up their "answer sheets". The app scans the images and then lets you know what percentage of the class answered the question correctly.

This tool is a bit more physical than the others. Not that holding up a paper is difficult, but the act of choosing which side of the paper belongs on top to correspond to the answer and holding the paper so that it's visible to the teacher's device makes it a different experience than simply holding a phone. I find this activity to be especially useful in early-morning classes when the students are still struggling to wake up!

www.get.plickers.com

Many of these tools are more alike than different. I suggest playing around with each to see which one you feel would work the best for your classroom on any given day. I find that students are appreciative of instructors simply trying new things, so you have nothing to lose!

CHAPTER 7
Tips For Engaging Classroom Discussions

Most college courses have an element of discussions in them, yet not all discussions are created equally. The instructor might not know how to ask questions effectively, the students might not know the material well, or it could be early on a Monday morning and everyone is still trying to wake up.

Another variable: your classroom might contain up to 50 percent introverts, which means they are thinking even if they're not talking. In what ways can an engaging instructor make classroom discussions meaningful, relevant and inviting to all students? Technology can help.

Kahoot Surveys

We've talked about using Kahoot for formative assessments in class. Kahoot has additional features other than quizzes, for instance surveys. You can set up a Kahoot survey much like a quiz, but instead of "correct" or "incorrect" answers you get a summary of the responses.

In my media course, we do a Kahoot survey on "News Attitudes". In this way, I can find out what my students consider news and where they obtain it. This process enables students to give authentic information without embarrassment (many of my students consume zero news and might be hesitant to say that to an instructor).

I have also used Kahoot surveys to find out what my students actually think about their use of social media. Many of them might not admit the extent of their use, but the authentic information provided by these surveys provide an excellent starting off point for discussions.

Kahoot surveys are also a great way for introverts to have their voices heard without having to speak in front of the group. When setting up Kahoot surveys, I encourage you to set a rather large response time in order to give all students time to consider their responses. Also remember that Kahoots can be used on many different devices, a phone is not required.

www.kahoot.com

Flipgrid

Flipgrid is an excellent way to have class discussions outside of class. Here's how it works: you post a question on the site and then share a code with the class. Once the class goes to the Flipgrid site and enters a code, they are able to video their own response to your question. I've used Flipgrid within class before so the students can see how it works, then later I've assigned Flipgrid discussions as homework.

The student can video their response as many times as they need to until they are comfortable with it. They can do it in the comfort of their own home. They can take time to formulate their responses. They can jazz up their video with stickers and emojis. Their responses are visible to the rest of the class, but you can edit the settings so that only people with the code can see your student's responses.

Flipgrid enables introverted students to give thoughtful responses in a creative way while enabling all students to show their personalities a bit. My students have loved the Flipgrids we have done and say they enjoy the community feeling it provides.

I've also discovered that Flipgrid is an excellent way to learn student names at the beginning of the term. Simply assign a Flipgrid for them to introduce themselves and you have a permanent record of their names and faces!

https://info.flipgrid.com/

Name-Choosing Apps

We've discussed earlier how sometimes the Hermoine Grangers of the classroom tend to dominate class discussions. Yet calling out unsuspecting students seems extreme. What's the solution? Decision apps are one option. It is the digital equivalent of drawing names out of a hat.

These apps are similar to a site called "Wheel Decide," which was actually created by co-workers who could never decide what type of food to have for lunch. On this site, you enter possibilities and then "spin the wheel", and the decision is made for you. I've used Wheel Decide in class before, but I have found that apps make the process a bit more streamlined because I can use my phone rather than my laptop.

Enter the names of your students on one of these apps. When a discussion starts to lag, simply grab your phone and open one of the apps. I use the free app "WhosNext" which works very similarly to Wheel Decide. I've even had one of my students activate the app, which is quite fun because the wheel starts to spin when you shake the phone. After a set amount of time, the app settles on a name.

It's important to announce to students that you're about to employ this tactic so you don't catch them off guard. It's also important to set the timing of the "spinning" high enough so that if the circle ends up stopping on the name of an introvert, they've had enough time to formulate a response. (Remember, introverts come up with great responses, just not as quickly as Hermoine.)

https://wheeldecide.com

https://miniwebtool.com/random-name-picker/

App: Tiny Decisions

App: Who's Next

Dice

This might seem very low-tech compared to other suggestions in this chapter, but I can't recommend this tip enough for early morning classes. Have the students pair up and give each pair of students one die. The post six questions to get the class period started. Instruct the students to take turn rolling the dice and answer the question that corresponds with the number they have rolled.

The point of this exercise is to get them awake and get them talking without it being a full classroom discussion. The introverts can chime in at their own pace, and the set-up is less intimidating than a discussion involving the entire room.

Once you've surmised that the students have gone through each of the questions, then open the floor up for pairs of students to share their responses. This is a great warm-up activity, it gets them talking to each other, and it lets *you* gauge how you think the rest of class is going to go.

Voxer

Have you ever had a class discussion that you wish could continue long after class had finished? The app Voxer gives you that opportunity.

Voxer is a walkie-talkie type app, where one can leave asynchronous voice messages for people or groups of people. Simply press a button and speak. Your message will be played by recipients at their leisure, and they can respond.

I've encouraged my students to use Voxer to reach out to me after class if they prefer to speak rather than email. It's also an excellent tool for shy or introverted students to ask me a question if they're not comfortable speaking to me after class. There have been times when I've received a question via Voxer on the way to the car at the end of the day, and I've been able to respond and answer before I even leave campus.

The real beauty of Voxer, however, is in the group function. If each student in a particular class or group has downloaded the free app, you can create a Voxer group and make each of them a member of that group.

Tips for Engaging Classroom Discussions

When one of the students sends a Voxer message to the group, it is available for all members of the group to listen and to respond. Students have told me that Voxer discussions (while never required in my courses – they typically occur organically) are particularly meaningful to them because they have the time to generate thoughtful responses and can reply on their own terms...from the comfort of their own rooms or anywhere else they might be outside the classroom.

This is a creative way for discussions to continue long after class has ended. And isn't this what we want – for students to engage in our material even outside the classroom?

www.voxer.com

Twitter

Thirty-nine percent of adults in the U.S. between ages 18-29 use Twitter. I have used Twitter in the classroom to generate and facilitate classroom discussions in a silent room to very satisfying results. That being said, there are studies that cite negative aspects of social media in the classroom, including information overload and inappropriate usage. If you're not familiar with Twitter, the "@" represents a user's name and the "#" represents a topic being mentioned in the tweet, or post.

I encourage my students to follow me on Twitter since I tweet daily about our class topics. I do not require it, however. I also tell them that I will not follow them on the platform unless they ask me specifically to do so after the term is over.

When using a hashtag, however, we can have discussions on Twitter without following each other. Say your course number is MEDC 1630. Simply tweet out a discussion question including the tag of your course: #MEDC1630. Hashtags must not have any special characters or spaces.

The students then follow the tag on Twitter, and anyone who responds to your question using the same tag (#MEDC1630) will show up on the search. This enables everyone in the class to contribute, their answers are public even though they may not have used their voices.

In a classroom discussion on Twitter, you will see your introverts come to life. You will discover how creative and clever some of those students in the back row can be. They enjoy using the platform, they enjoy using their devices in the classroom, and they enjoy a teacher who attempts new techniques to hear all voices.

There are two great websites that I use when doing Twitter class discussions: TwitterFall and TweetBeam. When you're using Twitter, you typically have to refresh your notifications in order to see the latest tweets that contain your class hashtag. TwitterFall and TweetBeam refresh automatically, and show the tweets containing the hashtag in sequential order. These sites are also free and make following the online discussion much easier.

"I like when professors use interactive apps, websites and other resources to make students get involved in class. I retain more knowledge and it makes me a more successful student."
– Matthew Zahn

www.twitter.com

www.twitterfall.com

www.tweetbeam.com

CHAPTER 8
Closing Thoughts

It has never been more important to be an engaging college instructor. It is my hope that the ideas in this book not only increase student success in your classrooms, but also increase your enjoyment of teaching. Whether you choose tech tools or not, your students will appreciate your efforts and you will realize that there's so much more to higher education teaching than the standard lecture with PowerPoint slides.

Here's to increased engagement, retention and enjoyment!

RESOURCES

For Adjuncts: Engaging With Other Engaging Adjuncts

Do you ever feel out of the loop? Are you exhausted with your "office" being your car? You are not alone. There are countless resources for you to reach out and connect with other adjuncts for support and camaraderie.

Check out websites like AdjunctNation (www.adjunctnation. com) or the SubReddit for adjuncts (https://www.reddit.com/r/ Adjuncts/). There is also an online group through Chronicle Vitae https://chroniclevitae.com/groups/adjunct-life.

www.adjunctnation.com

https://www.reddit.com/r/Adjuncts/

There are two groups on LinkedIn for adjuncts. One is called "Higher Education Adjunct Faculty" and the other is called "The Adjunct Network." The Facebook groups for adjuncts include "AdjunctNation" and "Adjunct World."

There are also several hashtags on Twitter worth following: #adjunctchat and #academicTwitter include many useful resources and ideas.

Further Reading

A Handbook For Adjunct/Part-Time Faculty And Teachers Of Adults, 7th Edition by Donald Greive, Ed.D. & Patricia Lesko, MFA. The Part-TimePress, 2015.

Handbook II – Advanced Teaching Strategies For Adjunct And Part-Time Faculty, 4th Edition by Donald Greive, Ed.D. & Patricia Lesko, MFA. The Part-TimePress, 2016.

Teach Like a Pirate by Dave Burgess, 2012, Dave Burgess Consulting.

COPYRIGHT FAIR USE GUIDELINES FOR COLLEGE FACULTY

What Types of Creative Work Does Copyright Protect?

Copyright protects works such as poetry, movies, CD-ROMs, video games, videos, plays, paintings, sheet music, recorded music performances, novels, software code, sculptures, photographs, choreography and architectural designs.

To qualify for copyright protection, a work must be "fixed in a tangible medium of expression." This means that the work must exist in some physical form for at least some period of time, no matter how brief. Virtually any form of expression will qualify as a tangible medium, including a computer's random access memory (RAM), the recording media that capture all radio and television broadcasts, and the scribbled notes on the back of an envelope that contain the basis for an impromptu speech.

In addition, the work must be original — that is, independently created by the author. It doesn't matter if an author's creation is similar to existing works, or even if it is arguably lacking in quality, ingenuity or aesthetic merit. So long as the author toils without copying from someone else, the results are protected by copyright.

Permission: What Is It and Why Do I Need It?

Obtaining copyright permission is the process of getting consent from a copyright owner to use the owner's creative material. Obtaining permission is often called "licensing"; when you have permission, you have a license to use the work. Permission is often (but not always) required because of intellectual property laws that protect creative works such as text, artwork, or music. (These laws are explained in more detail in the next section.) If you use a copyrighted work without the appropriate permission, you may be violating—or "infringing"—the owner's rights to that work. Infringing someone else's copyright may subject you to legal action. As if going to court weren't bad enough, you could be forced to stop using the work or pay money damages to the copyright owner.

As noted above, permission is not always required. In some situations, you can reproduce a photograph, a song, or text without a license. Generally, this will be true if the work has fallen into the public domain, or if your use qualifies as what's called a "fair use." Both of these legal concepts involve quite specific rules and are discussed more fully in subsequent chapters. In most cases, however, permission is required, so it's important to never assume that it's okay to use a work without permission.

Many people operate illegally, either intentionally or through ignorance. They use other people's work and never seek consent. This may work well for those who fly under the radar—that is, if copyright owners never learn of the use, or don't care enough to take action.

Obtaining Clearance for Coursepacks

It's the instructor's obligation to obtain clearance for materials used in class. Instructors typically delegate this task to one of the following:

- Clearance services. These services are the easiest method of clearance and assembly.

- University bookstores or copy shops. University policies may require that the instructor delegate the task to the campus bookstore, copy shop, or to a special division of the university that specializes in clearances.

Using a Clearance Service

It can be time-consuming to seek and obtain permission for the 20, 30, or more articles you want to use in a coursepack. Fortunately, private clearance services will, for a fee, acquire permission and assemble coursepacks on your behalf. After the coursepacks are created and sold, the clearance service collects royalties and distributes the payments to the rights holders. Educational institutions may require that the instructor use a specific clearance service. Some clearance companies also provide clearance for nonpaper electronic course-packs used in distance learning.

The largest copyright clearing service is the Copyright Clearance Center (www.copyright.com), which clears millions of works from thousands of publishers and authors.

In 2001, XanEdu (www.xanedu.com), acquired the coursepack service formerly known as Campus Custom Publishing. In addition to providing traditional coursepack assembly, XanEdu offers an electronic online service that provides supplemental college course materials directly to the instructor's desktop via the Internet.

Educational Uses of Non-coursepack Materials

Unlike academic coursepacks, other copyrighted materials can be used without permission in certain educational circumstances under copyright law or as a fair use. "Fair use" is the right to use portions of copyrighted materials without permission for purposes of education, commentary, or parody.

The Code of Best Practices in Fair Use for Media Literacy Education

In 2008, the Center for Media and Social Impact, in connection with American University, unveiled a guide of fair use practices for instructors in K–12 education, in higher education, in nonprofit organizations that offer programs for children and youth, and in adult education. The guide identifies five principles that represent acceptable practices for the fair use of copyrighted materials. You can learn more at the center's website, (www.cmsimpact.org).

Guidelines Establish a Minimum, Not a Maximum

In a case alleging 75 instances of infringement in an educational setting, 70 instances were not infringing because of fair use and for other reasons. The infringements were alleged because of the posting of copyrighted books within a university's e-reserve system. The court viewed the Copyright Office's 1976 Guidelines for Educational Fair Use as a minimum, not a maximum standard. The court then proposed its own fair use standard—10% of a book with less than ten chapters, or of a book that is not divided into chapters, or no more than one chapter or its equivalent in a book of more than ten chapters.—*Cambridge University Press v. Georgia State University*, Case 1:08-cv-01425-OD (N.D. Ga., May 11, 2012).

What is the Difference Between the Guidelines and Fair Use Principles?

The educational guidelines are similar to a treaty that has been adopted by copyright owners and academics. Under this arrangement, copyright owners will permit uses that are outlined in the guidelines. In other fair use situations, the only way to prove that a use is permitted is to submit the matter to court or arbitration. In other words, in order to avoid lawsuits, the various parties have agreed on what is permissible for educational uses, codified in these guidelines.

What is an "Educational Use?"

The educational fair use guidelines apply to material used in educational institutions and for educational purposes. Examples of "educational institutions" include K-12 schools, colleges, and universities. Libraries, museums, hospitals, and other nonprofit institutions also are considered educational institutions under most educational fair use guidelines when they engage in nonprofit instructional, research, or scholarly activities for educational purposes.

"Educational purposes" are:

* noncommercial instruction or curriculum-based teaching by educators to students at nonprofit educational institutions

* planned noncommercial study or investigation directed toward making a contribution to a field of knowledge, or

* presentation of research findings at noncommercial peer conferences, workshops, or seminars.

Rules for Reproducing Text Materials

The guidelines permit a teacher to make one copy of any of the following: a chapter from a book; an article from a periodical or newspaper; a short story, short essay, or short poem; a chart, graph, diagram, drawing, cartoon, or picture from a book, periodical, or newspaper.

Teachers may not photocopy workbooks, texts, standardized tests, or other materials that were created for educational use. The guidelines were not intended to allow teachers to usurp the profits of educational publishers. In other words, educational publishers do not consider it a fair use if the copying provides replacements or substitutes for the purchase of books, reprints, periodicals, tests, workbooks, anthologies, compilations, or collective works.

Rules for Reproducing Music

A music instructor can make copies of excerpts of sheet music or other printed works, provided that the excerpts do not constitute a "performable unit," such as a whole song, section, movement, or aria. In no case can more than 10% of the whole work be copied and the number of copies may not exceed one copy per pupil. Printed copies that have been purchased may be edited or simplified provided that the fundamental character of the work is not distorted or the lyrics altered (or added to).

A student may make a single recording of a performance of copyrighted music for evaluation or rehearsal purposes, and the educational institution or individual teacher may keep a copy. In addition, a single copy of a sound recording owned by an educational institution or an individual teacher (such as a tape, disc, or cassette) of copyrighted music may be made for the purpose of constructing aural exercises or examinations, and the educational institution or individual teacher can keep a copy.

Rules for Recording and Showing Television Programs

Nonprofit educational institutions can record television programs transmitted by network television and cable stations. The institution can keep the tape for 45 days, but can only use it for instructional purposes during the first ten of the 45 days. After the first ten days, the video recording can only be used for teacher evaluation purposes, to determine whether or not to include the broadcast program in the teaching curriculum. If the teacher wants to keep it within the curriculum, he or she must obtain permission from the copyright owner. The recording may be played once by each individual teacher in the course of related teaching activities in classrooms and similar places devoted to instruction (including formalized home instruction). The recorded program can be repeated once if necessary, although there are no standards for determining what is and is not necessary. After 45 days, the recording must be erased or destroyed.

A video recording of a broadcast can be made only at the request of and only used by individual teachers. A television show may not be regularly recorded in anticipation of requests—for example, a teacher cannot make a standing request to record each episode of a PBS series. Only enough copies may be reproduced from each recording to meet the needs of teachers, and the recordings may not be combined to create teaching compilations. All copies of a recording must include the copyright notice on the broadcast program as recorded and (as mentioned above) must be erased or destroyed after 45 days.

Stanford Copyright and Fair Use Center, Stanford University Libraries, Stanfold University, 2017 (http://fairuse.stanford.edu/).

References

Abilock, Debbie, and Connie Williams. "Recipe For An Info-graphic." Knowledge Quest 43.2 (2014): 46-55. Academic Search Complete. Web. 28 Jan. 2017.

Ahmad, Tunku, Frank Doheny, Sheila Faherty, and Nuala Harding. "How Instructor-Developed Screencasts Benefit College Students' Learning of Maths: Insights from an Irish Case Study." The Malaysian Online Journal of Educational Technology 1.4 (n.d.): 12-25, 2013. Print.

Al-Jarf, Reima. "Enhancing freshman students' writing skills with a mind-mapping software." Conference proceedings of eLearning and Software for Education (eLSE). Issue no.01 /2009, pp. 375-382. Bucharest, Romania.

Averianova, Irina, and European Association For Computer-Assisted Language Learning (EUROCALL) (United Kingdom). A Cell Phone in the Classroom: A Friend or a Foe? N.p.: European Association for Computer-Assisted Language Learning (EUROCALL), 2012. ERIC. Web. 27 Jan. 2017.

Ball, Christy. "Sparking Passion: Engaging Student Voice Through Project-Based Learning in Learning Communities." Learning Communities Research & Practice 9th ser. 4.1 (2016): 1-6. Print.

Berk, Ronald A. "How to Create 'Thriller' PowerPoints® in the Classroom!" Innovative Higher Education 37.2 (2011): 141-52. Print.

Berry, M. J., & Westfall, A. (2015). Dial D for Distraction: The Making and Breaking of Cell Phone Policies in the College Classroom. College Teaching, 63(2), 62–71.

Boag, C. (1989). What makes a good teacher? The Bulletin, July 18, p.46-52

Bright, Suzanne. "I share my own experiences in the classroom, in school leadership, and in my work in professional development. I share both my successes and my failures and how I responded to both, so that students see the value in being reflective and continuing to learn and grow throughout your career." 6 August 2017, 10:05 a.m. Facebook post.

References

Burgess, D. (2012). Teach Like a Pirate. Dave Burgess Consulting, Incorporated.

Byrne, John. "Learning and Memory (Section 4, Chapter 7) Neuroscience Online: An Electronic for the Neurosciences | Department of Neurobiology and Anatomy - The University of Texas Medical School at Houston." Learning and Memory (Section 4, Chapter 7) Neuroscience Online: An Electronic Textbook for the Neurosciences | Department of Neurobiology and Anatomy - The University of Texas Medical School at Houston. University of Texas McGovern Medical School, n.d. Web. 13 Apr. 2017.

Carey, Benedict. "Brain Science for Beginners." Independent School 75.1 (2015): 88-91. Print.

Cavanaugh, Sean. "Popular Songs to Engage Students? Play Tunes in Class, Says Music School Dean." Edweek Marketbrief. EdWeek, 10 Mar. 2015. Web. 26 Jan. 2017. <https://marketbrief.edweek.org/marketplace-k-12/popular_songs_to_engage_students_play_tunes_in_class/>.

Christenbury, L. 2010. "The Flexible Teacher." The Effective Educator 68 (4): 46–50.

Chickering, A. W., and Z. F. Gamson. 1987. "Seven Principles for Good Practice in Undergraduate Education." AAHE Bulletin 39 (7): 3–7

Choy, S. Chee, Pauline Swee Choo Goh, and Daljeet Singh Sedhu. "How and Why Students Learn: Development and Validation of the Learner Awareness Levels Questionnaire for Higher Education Students." International Journal of Teaching and Learning in Higher Education 28.1 (2016): 94-101. Print.

Collins English Dictionary – Complete and Unabridged, 12th Edition 2014. S.v. "recency effect." Retrieved July 2 2017

Cook, Dani Brecher, and Kevin Michael Klipfel. "How Do Our Students Learn? An Outline of a Cognitive Psychological Model for Information Literacy Instruction." Reference & User Services Quarterly 55.1 (2015): 34. Print.

Cooper, James L., Jean Macgregor, Karl A. Smith, and Pamela Robinson. "Implementing Small-Group Instruction: Insights from Successful Practitioners." New Directions for Teaching and Learning 2000.81 (2000): 63-76. Print.

Couros, George. The Innovators Mindset Empower Learning, Unleash Talent, and Lead a Culture of Creativity. Dave Burgess Consulting, 2015.

Crosling, Glenda, Margaret Heagney, and Liz Thomas. "Improving Student Retention in Higher Education." Australian Universities' Review 51.2 (2009): 9-18. Print.

Davis, Barbara Gross. Tools for Teaching. San Francisco: Jossey-Bass, 1993. Print.

Diamond, Marian Cleeves., and Janet L. Hopson. Magic Trees of the Mind: How to Nurture Your Child's Intelligence, Creativity, and Healthy Emotions from Birth through Adolescence. New York: Dutton, 1998. Print.

Doyle, Terry. Helping Students Learn in a Learner-centered Environment: A Guide to Facilitating Learning in Higher Education. Sterling, VA: Stylus Pub., 2008. Print.

Elwick, Alex, ed. "Can Learning about the Brain Transform Pupils' Motivation to Learn." An Awareness of Neuroscience in Education: CfBT Education Trust (2014): n. pag. Print.

Evans, C. (2014). Twitter for teaching: Can social media be used to enhance the process of learning? British Journal of Educational Technology, 45, 902-915. doi:10.1111/bjet.12099

Farrand, P A. "The efficacy of the `mind map' study technique." Medical Education (2002): 426-431. Print.

Fathima, M. Parimala, N. Sasikumar, and M. Panimalar Roja. "Memory and Learning - A Study from Neurological Perspective." iManager's Journal on Educational Psychology5.4 (2012): 9-14. Print.

Freidman, T. "How to Get a Job at Google." New York Times, Feb., 23, 2014, Section SR, Page 11.

Freire, Paolo. Pedagogy of the Oppressed. Verlag Herder, 1968.

Frey, T. K., & Tatum, N. T. (2016). The Influence of Classroom Cell Phone Policies on Instructor Credibility. Journal of the Communication, Speech & Theatre Association of North Dakota, 29, 1–13.

George, Daniel R., Tomi D. Dreibelbis, and Betsy Aumiller. "How We Used Two Social Media Tools To Enhance Aspects Of Active Learning During Lectures." Medical Teacher

35.12 (2013): 985-988. Academic Search Complete. Web. 28 Jan. 2017.

Glass, A., Holyoak, K. Cognition. McGraw-Hill Ryerson, Limited, 1986.

Hardman, J. (2016) Opening-Up Classroom Discourse to Promote and Enhance Active, Collaborative and Cognitively-Engaging Student Learning Experiences. In C. Goria, O. Speicher, & S. Stollhans (Eds.), Innovative Language Teaching and Learning at University: Enhancing Participation and Collaboration (pp. 5-16). Dublin: Research-Publishing.net

Heider, Joseph. "Using Digital Learning Solutions To Address Higher Education's Greatest Challenges." Publishing Research Quarterly 31.3 (2015): 183-189. Academic Search Complete. Web. 28 Jan. 2017.

Hughes, Brian. "Are Infographics Dead?" Social Media Today, 9 Oct. 2015, www.socialmediatoday.com/marketing/brian-hughes/2015-10-09/are-infographics-dead.

Jalali, Alireza, Jacqueline Carnegie, Maxwell Hincke, Rong Sun, Martin Gauthier, and John Leddy. Use of Podcasting as an Innovative Asynchronous E-Learning Tool for Students. 2011. Print.

Jankowski, Natasha. United States. American Council on Education Leadership and Advocacy. Unpacking Relationships. 2016.

Kahn, Peter E. "Theorising Student Engagement in Higher Education." British Educational Research Journal 40.6 (2013): 1005-018. Print.

Kambel, Danny (DannyKambel) 'In my opinion, authenticity is found in accountability and responsibility'. 6 August 2017, 7:22 a.m. Tweet.

King, Alison. "From Sage on the Stage to Guide on the Side." College Teaching 41.1 (1993): 30-35. Print.

King, Paul. "How Does the Human Brain Decide Which Memories to Store."Https://www.quora.com/How-does-the-human-brain-decide-which-memories-to-store#. Quora, 6 Aug. 2016. Web. 13 Apr. 2017.

Kivunja, Charles. "Innovative Pedagogies in Higher Education to Become Effective Teachers of 21st Century Skills: Unpacking the Learning and Innovations Skills Domain of the New Learning Paradigm." International Journal of Higher Education 3.4 (2014). Print.

Kohn, A. Feel-bad Education: The Cult of Rigor and the Loss of Joy. Education Week, October 1, 2004. 24.

Kuh, George D., Ty M. Cruce, Rick Shoup, Jillian Kinzie, and Robert M. Gonyea. "Unmasking the Effects of Student Engagement on First-Year College Grades and Persistence." The Journal of Higher Education 79.5 (2008): 540-63. Print.

Kunter, Mareike, Yi-Miau Tsai, Uta Klusmann, Martin Brunner, Stefan Krauss, and Jürgen Baumert. "Students' and Mathematics Teachers' Perceptions of Teacher Enthusiasm and Instruction." Learning and Instruction 18.5 (2008): 468-82. Print.

LaFlamme, Art. "1) bringing in real world examples and experiences and 2) taking the lessons and materials and directly connecting them to what they see around them. Through examples and evidence, abstract concepts aren't that anymore" 6 August 2017, 9:40 a.m. Facebook post.

LaFlamme, Art. "Every instructor should be able to hand their CV to their students. Here is my basis for instructing you, and not have a student flinch. It's not salesmanship, it's basis of expertise. Students do not want an instructor who is, so to speak, back on their heels but one who is forward on their toes, working hard to support their learning. Every moment, every day" 6 August 2017, 9:55 a.m. Facebook post.

Lancaster, A. L. (2018). Student Learning with Permissive and Restrictive Cell Phone Policies: A Classroom Experiment. International Journal for the Scholarship of Teaching and Learning, 12(1).

Lave, Jean. (2011). Changing Practice, Mind, Culture, and Activity, 19:2, 156-171. https://www.tandfonline.com/doi/abs/10.1080/10749039.2012.666317

Lave, Jean. Learning as a Socially Situated Activity. Perf. GSI Teaching and Resource Center, 2011. Web. 25 Jan. 2017. <https://vimeo.com/22409249>.

References

Lei, S.,D. Donoso, K. Foutz, M. Lasorsa, and S. Oliver. "Forgetting to Remember Important Course Information: Instructors' Perspectives." College Student Journal 45.1 (2011): 36-46. Print.

Lenhart, A. (2010). Cell phones and American adults: They make just as many calls, but text less often than teens. Pew Internet & American Life Project. Retrieved from http://www.pewinternet.org/media//Files/Reports/2010/PIP_Adults_Cellphones_Report_2010.pdf

Lipp, Genevieve. "Kahoot! as Formative Assessment." Center for Instructional Technology. Web. 28 Jan. 2017.

Litemind. (2012). "What is Mindmapping (and How to Get Started)," from https://litemind.com/what-is-mind-mapping/.

Lobel, Thalma. Sensation: The New Science of Physical Intelligence. New York: Atria, 2014. Print.

Lumpkin, Angela, Rebecca Achen, and Regan Dodd. "Student Perceptions of Active Learning." College Student Journal 49.1 (2015): 121-33. Print.

Macknight, A. D. C. "Adventures in Education." Advances in Physiology Education 40.3 (2016): 377-82. Print.

Mandernach, Jean, PhD. "Assessment of Student Engagement in Higher Education: A Synthesis of Literature and Assessment Tools." International Journal of Teaching and Learning in Higher Education 12.2 (2015): 1-14. Print.

Mangan, Katherine. "The Personal Lecture." Chronicle of Higher Education 09 Dec. 2016: A8+. Academic Search Complete. Web. 28 Jan. 2017.

Marland, Perc. Learning to Teach: A Primer for Pre-service Teachers. Frenchs Forest, N.S.W.: Pearson Education Australia, 2007. Print.

McMillan, Wendy Jayne. "'Your Thrust Is to Understand' – How Academically Successful Students Learn." Teaching in Higher Education 15.1 (2010): 1-13. Print.

Morrison, Kristan. "Making Teacher Education More Democratic: Incorporating Student Voice and Choice, Part Two." Educational Horizons 87.2 (2009): 102-15. Print.

Nilson, Linda Burzotta. Teaching at Its Best: A Research-based Resource for College Instructors. —, MA: Anker Pub., 2003. Print.

Palmer, Betsy, et al. "Undergraduates, Technology, And Social Connections." College Student Journal 48.2 (2014): 281-296. Academic Search Complete. Web. 28 Jan. 2017.

Park, Elisa L., and Bo Keum Choi. "Transformation of Classroom Spaces: Traditional versus Active Learning Classroom in Colleges." Higher Education 68.5 (2014): 749-71. Print.

Pasinski, Marie, and Jodie Gould. Beautiful Brain, Beautiful You: Look Radiant from the inside out by Empowering Your Mind. New York: Hyperion, 2011. Print.

Rhodes, Gary. "Faculty Engagement to Enhance Student Attainment." Paper prepared for National Commission on Higher Education Attainment, 2012, from https://www.acenet.edu/Documents/Faculty-Engagement-to-Enhance-Student-Attainment--Rhoades.pdf.

Ricoy, María-Carmen, and Tiberio Feliz. "Twitter As A Learning Community In Higher Education." Journal Of Educational Technology & Society 19.1 (2016): 237-248. Academic Search Complete. Web. 28 Jan. 2017.

Riley, Benjamin. "The Value of Knowing How Students Learn." Phi Delta Kappan 97.7 (2016): 35-38. Print.

Robinson, Sir Ken. "Do Schools Kill Creativity?" Sir Ken Robinson at TED, 2006. https://www.youtube.com/watch?v=Ue9sAoFcyOU

Robinson, Sir Ken. How To Escape Education's Death Valley. Perf. How to Escape Education's Death Valley. TED Talk, Apr. 2014. Web. 22 Jan. 2017.

Rudd, J., and M. J. Rudd. "Coping with Information Load: User Strategies and Implications for Librarians." College & Research Libraries 47.4 (1986): 315-22. Print.

Sack-Minn, Joetta. "Social Media Helps Educators Build Professional Learning Communities." Education Digest Feb. 2017: 25-29. Print.

Schwartz, Katrina. "Making Learning Visible: Doodling Helps Memories Stick." MindShift. Web. 26 Jan. 2017.

References

Severiens, Sabine, Marieke Meeuwisse, and Marise Born. "Student Experience And Academic Success: Comparing A Student-Centred And A Lecture-Based Course Programme." Higher Education 70.1 (2015): 1-17. Academic Search Complete. Web. 28 Jan. 2017.

Short, Fay, and Jesse Martin. "Presentation vs. Performance: Effects of Lecturing Style in Higher Education on Student Preference and Student Learning." Psychology Teaching Review 17.2 (2011): 71-82. Print.

Simonds, Katie. "I'm Seventeen." TEDx Boise, 9 Feb. 2015, www.youtube.com/watch?v=0OkOQhXhsIE.

"Small Changes in Teaching: The First 5 Minutes of Class." The Chronicle of Higher Education. 11 Jan. 2016. Web. 26 Jan. 2017.

Stormon-Flynn, Mary. "Getting and Keeping Students' Brains Energized and Eager." Thesis. Gordon College, 2011. Print.

Taylor, Mark. "Leveraging Social Media For Instructional Goals: Status, Possibilities, And Concerns." New Directions For Teaching & Learning 2015.144 (2015): 37-46. Academic Search Complete. Web. 28 Jan. 2017.

Tews, Michael J., Kathy Jackson, Crystal Ramsay, and John W. Michel. "Fun in the College Classroom: Examining Its Nature and Relationship with Student Engagement." College Teaching 63.1 (2015): 16-26. Print.

Therrell, James and Dunneback, Staci. "What Is Important to Students?" Journal of the Scholarship of Teaching and Learning 15.5 (2015): 49. Print.

Thomas, Kevin M., Blanche W. O'Bannon, and Natalie Bolton. "Cell Phones in the Classroom: Teachers' Perspectives of Inclusion, Benefits, and Barriers." Computers in the Schools 30.4 (2013): 295-308. Print.

Umbach, P. D., Wawrzynski, M. R. Faculty do Matter: The Role of College Faculty in Student Learning and Engagement. Research in Higher Education 46, 153–184 (2005). https://doi.org/10.1007/s11162-004-1598-1.

Wammes, Jeffrey D., Melissa E. Meade, and Myra A. Fernandes. "The Drawing Effect: Evidence for Reliable and Robust Memory Benefits in Free Recall." The Quarterly Journal of Experimental Psychology 69.9 (2016): 1752-776. Print.

Wang, Xiaoyan, Yelin Su, Stephen Cheung, Eva Wong, and Theresa Kwong. "An Exploration of Biggs' Constructive Alignment in Course Design and Its Impact on Students' Learning Approaches." Assessment & Evaluation in Higher Education 38.4 (2013): 477-91. Print.

Wenglinsky, H. (2000) How Teaching Matters: Bringing the Classroom Back into Discussions of Teacher Quality. Princeton, NJ: Policy Information Center

Whittaker, Todd. "Keynote Address." Connecting the Four Cs Conference. 7 June 2017, Mount Vernon, Indiana.

Wieman, Carl. "A Better Way to Evaluate Undergraduate Teaching." Change: The Magazine of Higher Learning 47.1 (2015): 6-15. Print.

Willis, J. "The Neuroscience of Joyful Education." Educational Leadership 64 (2007).

Wolpert-Gawron, Heather. "What the Heck Is Project-Based Learning?" Edutopia. George Lucas Educational Foundation, 26 Jan. 2015. Web. 02 July 2017.

Index

P

Padlet 60, 61. *See* online poster
padlet.com 59
paper.li 81
Park, E. 36
participatory teaching 53
Pasinski, M. 35
PearlTrees 81
pearltrees.com 81
Pechakucha 70. *See* presentation tools
piktochart.com 72
Plickers 84
podbean.com 75
podcasting tools 73, 74
podomatic.com 75
PollEverywhere 67
polleverywhere.com 68
postermywall.com 60
PowerPoint 8, 30, 31, 70, 74
prefrontal cortex 13, 14
presentation tools 70
Prezi 70. *See* presentation tools
professional development 11, 12, 46
Project Based Learning 40. *See* questioning techniques

Q

QR codes 4, 33, 67
questioning 31, 32. *See also* questioning techniques
questioning techniques 31
Quizizz 79

R

Ramsay, C. 52
Reddit 94
Reed, Anne 42
remind.com 61
Rhodes, G. 19
Riley, B. 13
risk-taking 48
Robinson, P. 38
Robinson, Sir Ken 14
Roja, M.P. 14
Rudd, M.J. 34

S

sage on the stage 9, 20, 23
Sasikumar, N. 14
Schopenhauer, Arthur 20
Schulman, Nev 69
Schwartz, K. 41

FAQ's...

How can I place an orders?

Orders can be placed **by mail** to Part-Time Press, P.O. Box 130117, Ann Arbor, MI 48113-0117, **by phone** or fax at (734)930-6854 and **online at** https://www.Part-TimePress.com.

How much do I pay if I want multiple copies?

Each Part-Time Press book has a quantity discount schedule available. The schedule for *Wake'Em Up* is:

1-9 copies--no discount   **10-49 copies**--10% discount

50-99 copies--20% discount **100 or more copies**--30% discount

How can I pay for orders?

Orders can be placed on **a purchase order** or can be paid by **check** or **credit card** (Visa/Mastercard, Discover or AMEX.)

How will my order be shipped?

Standard shipping to a continental U.S. street address is via **UPS-Ground Service**. Foreign shipments or U.S. post office box addresses go through the **U.S. Postal Service** and express shipments via **UPS-2nd Day**, or **UPS-Next Day**. Shipping and handling charges are based on the dollar amount of the shipment, and a fee schedule is shown on the next page.

What if I'm a reseller like a bookstore or wholesaler?

Resellers get a standard **20 percent discount** off of the single copy retail price, or may choose to receive the multiple copy discount.

Part-Time Press Books: Order Form

Qty	Title	Unit $$	Total
	Wake 'Em Up—Supercharging Student Engag.	**$20.00**	
	Handbook for Adjunct/Part-Time Faculty, 7th ed.	**$20.00**	
	Going the Distance: A Handbook for Part-Time & Adjunct Faculty Who Teach Online, 2nd ed.	**$15.00**	
	Teaching in the Sciences	**$20.00**	
	Excellent Online Science Teaching	**$20.00**	
	Teaching Strategies and Techniques, 6th ed.	**$15.00**	
	Handbook II: Advanced Teaching Strategies	**$20.00**	
	Blended Learning & Flipped Classrooms	**$20.00**	
		Subtotal	
		Shipping	
		Total	

Purchaser/Payment Information

☐   *Check (payable to The Part-Time Press)*

☐   *Credit Card # ———————————————— Exp. ————*

    CVV# ————

☐   *Purchase Order # ————————————————*

Name ———————————————————————

Institution ————————————————————————

Address ———————————— City/ST/Zip ——————————

Ph:———————————— E-mail: ————————————

Shipping Schedule:

1-4 books $6.00

5+ books   8 percent of the purchase price

Part-Time Press: P.O. Box 130117, Ann Arbor, MI 48113-0117
Fax: 734-930-6854 E-mail: orders@part-timepress.com
Order securely online: https://www.Part-TimePress.com